And we know that God causes everything to work together for the good of those who love God and are called according to His purpose for them.
- Romans 8:28

A BIGGER Purpose
Stories That Inspire

TRIBUTE PUBLISHING

2017

Copyright © 2017
Tribute Publishing, LLC
Frisco, Texas

Tribute Publishing, LLC

A Bigger Purpose
First Edition April 2017

All Worldwide Rights Reserved
ISBN: 978-0-998-2860-1-3

All Rights Reserved. No part of this book may be reproduced, stored in a retrieval system, or transmitted, in any form, or by any means, electronic, mechanical, recorded, photocopied, or otherwise, without the prior written permission of the copyright owner, except by a reviewer who may quote brief passages in a review.

In God We Trust

"My thoughts are nothing like your thoughts," says the Lord.
"And my ways are far beyond anything you could imagine.
- Isaiah 55:8

Contents

Prologue xi

Chapter 1 – Embracing Life's Experiences 1

Chapter 2 – The Power of Prayer 15

Chapter 3 – The Gift in You 41

Chapter 4 – Move Forward, Pursue Your Dream 55

Chapter 5 – A Life Well Lived 77

Chapter 6 – Are You Fully Equipped? 93

Epilogue 101

About Mike Rodriguez 105

Prologue

Many times I have been humbled with the opportunity to witness God's blessing and miracles. Whether in my own life or through the life of a family member, friend or someone else. I cannot and will not profess to know how or why God does what He does, He is after all, God. However, I do know that He is present and we can experience a glimpse of His love and compassion if we only get to know Him.

I decided to publish this book because I knew there were others like me who had a story to tell about God's amazing work. Others who had witnessed first-hand his blessings. Normal people like me and like you that had a story of faith to share.

The contributing authors in this book were brave enough to share their own stories and insights. They did this with the hope that other people, like you, would find something to take away. Something that would inspire you to make the important changes in your life. To understand that what you are going through does not define you, but can certainly refine you to start living with and for a bigger purpose. You can do it, however, you must be willing to believe, take action, and start pursuing your greatest purpose. I would like to tell you that it is going to be easy, but it is not. I would like to say that there is nothing special about the contributors to this book, but that would also not be true. Yet, it would also be false for you to believe that there is nothing special about you, too.

You were created with precision, purpose, and your own unique talents. You were also given the ability to know, act on, and use those talents to become great and strong in your own way. Just know, remember, and most importantly believe this, "I can do all things through Christ, who strengthens me." Philippians 4:13 (*NKJV*). As I always say, "Through faith and action, ALL things are possible."

Now, let's get YOU started on living for a bigger purpose.

Mike Rodriguez

"In Christ, we already have the victory, but in our life situations we often forget that."
- Jillian Murphy

Chapter 1

Embracing Life's Experiences
By Dr. Gary Adams

"There is a world of difference between knowing something to be true in your head and experiencing the reality in your life."

— Henry T. Blackaby, *Experiencing God*

In the 1970s, I went on a journey to Argentina to be with my parents who were missionaries there. They had invited me to conduct a conference for pastors and church workers, as well as to speak to local congregations personally. I was excited because this was my first trip to Argentina, and I felt honored to minister there. Argentina was experiencing a major revival at the time, and I was fully expecting God to allow me to be part of it.

I had learned from previous mission trips that I had taken to expect the unexpected. You never know ahead of time what God might do. So often I had come away from a missions

Chapter 1 – Embracing Life's Experiences

trip thanking God for the lives He touched through my ministry, but knowing that my life was enriched as much, if not more, than those to whom I had ministered.

One Sunday morning as my dad was filling me in on plans for that day, he informed me that we were going to minister at a small church high in the Andes Mountains and he said that the pastor of the church never had a North American minister in his church. According to my father, the pastor was overjoyed knowing that I would come to his church to speak. I would soon realize that I was there for what God was about to do in me as much as what He wanted to do for the people of this barren, arid region of the Andes.

We drove for a couple of hours through the majestic Andes before arriving at the little church. Upon arrival, I was introduced to the pastor, an elderly man whose face was etched with time. His weather-worn countenance, however, reflected not only the passage of time but also the presence of God in his life. I could tell just by being in his presence that this man knew God in a simple, trusting way, something I yearned for in my life. It was not as though I didn't know God, but when I got into the presence of this man who had walked with God for many years, there was a spiritual effect; a holy impact of sorts, that stirred my spirit.

I preached my message to a small crowd that had gathered in the drafty little building that morning. The people sat on split logs, eagerly taking in every word I spoke. I was elated to have such a receptive audience. The size of this church

Chapter 1 – Embracing Life's Experiences

didn't matter to me. There, way high in the Andes, was a little flock of God's people who were hungry for the Word of God. I thought to myself how rewarding this experience was. My heart was full; I was satisfied in a way that only God can satisfy. However, the best was yet to come.

Immediately following the meeting, we had planned to hurry back down the mountain to get to the church where I was scheduled to speak that evening. As I concluded my message and was bidding farewell to the people, I noticed my Dad was engaged in an intense discussion with the old pastor. Although far enough removed from them that I could not hear their conversation, I could see that the pastor was visibly upset. Tears filled his aged eyes. Rivulets of tears ran down the creases of his face. I was alarmed. "Dad, what is wrong?" I asked. All manner of thoughts ran through my mind. Had I said or done something to offend this godly man? I had to know. Dad gently led me aside and began to explain. He told me that the pastor had planned on honoring me by preparing lunch. Serving a meal was a customary way of honoring those who came to minister, but this was a super-special occasion for this pastor and his church since they had never had a North American come to minister to them.

My dad had told the pastor that due to our schedule, we would not be able to stay for lunch. And, he had explained that although honored by his invitation, if we stayed we wouldn't be able to get to our next engagement on time. It was at this point that the pastor had begun to weep. I asked

Chapter 1 – Embracing Life's Experiences

my Dad, "Is lunch that important to him?" He said, "Almost all this pastor owns is a lamb. This morning he had the lamb slaughtered and had it prepared for our lunch. It is his way of honoring you." He continued, "When I told him we could not stay, he began to weep as though his heart was broken." My mind was in a whirl. The idea that this pastor had sacrificed the only real thing he owned to bless and honor me was one of the most humbling experiences of my life. "Dad!" I exclaimed, "Tell him we will stay! I don't know how we will make it to the next meeting on time, but I cannot leave this pastor like this. Somehow, God will make a way!" Dad agreed, and as he conveyed our acceptance to stay for lunch, the old pastor lifted his head, raised his hands and began clapping for joy. He shouted, "Gloria a Dios, es hora de la fiesta!" Which translated means, "Glory to God, it's time to party!"

After an excellent meal, we made our way back down the mountain. Only God knows how, but we made it to the next meeting on time for me to speak. My heart was still full and overflowing, and I ministered from the overflow that night. After a long day of ministry, we headed back to my parents' home, where I was looking forward to a good rest. As I lay in bed, my mind went back over all the events of the day. I was trying to get some greatly needed sleep, but it was not coming. I began to think how God had taken His greatest possession, a Lamb, to offer to the world for whoever will accept Him. I wondered how many receiving His invitation turn Him down because they are too busy with life. Somehow taking time for the Lamb doesn't fit their busy

Chapter 1 – Embracing Life's Experiences

schedule. Others question, as I had, "Is it that important?" As I pondered these things, I began to realize more fully the impact of what it means to our Heavenly Father for us to accept the sacrifice of His Lamb, Jesus, the Son of God. The old pastor's willingness to give all he owned was an invaluable lesson in selflessness and sacrifice. Reflected through him I had seen a living expression of God's heart, who "so loved the world that He gave" His only son, Jesus. What if I had decided that I was too busy to accept the invitation? What if I had ignored the promptings of my heart to stay for this beautiful fiesta? What would have happened if I had fretted and complained because MY schedule was interrupted? What a dynamic experience I would have missed! The pastor's example left an indelible mark on my life. I knew my Heavenly Father was calling me to a new level of selflessness and sacrifice.

I never saw the old pastor again. My dad told me later that the pastor had died a few years after I was there, but he added, "The pastor never forgot you coming there." Perhaps it had been a dynamic experience for both of us!

Life is made of all types of experiences, some good and some not so good, but it is for certain that nobody goes through life without them. Experiences help make up the fabric of our lives. The way we respond to those experiences paint the colors of that fabric in different hues. Furthermore, knowing God through Jesus the Messiah gives us the brushes and the colors and gives Him the right to paint a beautiful mosaic. Experience is defined as "a practical contact with and

Chapter 1 – Embracing Life's Experiences

observation of facts or events." Involvement in, participation in, and observation of life events become our experiences; the way we view or respond to them can be a form of dynamic living. The most dynamic experiences are those of giving one's life to Jesus, letting Him live His life through you.

In my new book scheduled for release this spring, May 2017, I describe the significance of spiritual dynamics. Additionally, I define the dynamics of love, prayer, of faith, and forgiveness, as well as other forms of spiritual dynamics. Our response to each experience will help shape whether it becomes a positive dynamic in our life or the life of others. Even a seemingly bad experience can become a powerful and positive dynamic as we respond according to God's Word in prayer, love, and forgiveness. You must see experiences through God's eyes to realize the amazing things God is doing through these experiences.

One balmy evening while driving home from a class at the Bible College I was attending in Pensacola, Florida, I had an experience with what I would later come to believe is what the Bible describes as "walking in the Spirit." Simply stated, it means to walk with an awareness of God's presence, guidance, and involvement in everyday living. Not far from the college, I turned onto a busy street and saw a disabled vehicle in front of me, pulled to the curb under a street light. The hood of the small sports car was lifted, and a young man was peering into the engine space. I passed by, thinking nothing unusual. Just someone having car problems, I

Chapter 1 – Embracing Life's Experiences

thought. Shortly after I passed by, I heard a small inner voice saying, "Turn around, and go tell that man that I [God] love him." Well, now I was concerned. Never in my life had I been aware of an inner voice like that. One of my first thoughts was, "The guy will think I'm some nut." Then I desperately tried to convince myself that I obviously was having an overactive imagination. The thought persisted, and then that same small voice seemed to say to me, "If I asked you to do something gallant, you would do it wouldn't you?" When I committed my life to follow the Lord, I had told the Lord that I would do what He asked of me, go where He wanted me to go, and become who He wanted me to be. Now I was getting an opportunity to validate my commitment to the Lord.

I decided to obey the prompting of what must be the Holy Spirit speaking, even if it made me seem like a fool to a total stranger. I went around the block and came up behind the small car once again, noticing that the hood was now down. Just as I was pulling in behind him, the driver entered his car and pulled away from the curb. I was quite happy, feeling that I had passed a huge test on obeying God, I was planning to head on to my home. Well, that small voice came again saying, "You didn't do what I told you to do. You haven't told him that I love him." Speaking to myself, I reasoned, "The guy is already gone, it's getting late, and I need to get home." I was not only feeling apprehensive about the situation, but concerned that if this was, in fact, the Lord speaking to me, I had better obey. The voice persisted, "Follow him! You were a cop; you know how to tail him."

Chapter 1 – Embracing Life's Experiences

The thought crossed my mind that perhaps I was not lucid. After all, who in their right mind would follow a total stranger late at night on such a whim? Sensing that I needed to obey, I started tailing the guy. After a few miles, and several turns, it became apparent to me that the driver knew I was following him. He sped up, so I sped up. He turned, so I turned. He was apparently trying to shake me off; we continued for miles. My old "cop" mentality kicked in, so I now determined that I would not let him evade me. I was on a mission. We continued for a considerable time and distance until he finally pulled into an apartment complex, quickly skidded into a parking spot and bailed out of his car on a fast run toward some apartments. I slammed my brakes, jumped out of my car and yelled loud enough to wake everyone in the complex. "God said to tell you that he loves you!" I shouted loudly. The young man dropped to his knees and began crying. I walked over to him to explain my actions, but no other words would come. I had not been given anything else to say to him. I just repeated, "God loves you!" I thought I should probably go now, not knowing what else to say. I was relieved as the young man began to regain his composure and speak to me. What he said would have a lasting impact on me.

He said, "Sir, I have to tell you what just happened." He went on to say how that very morning he had decided that this would be his last day on earth. He was planning to take his life because he felt that nobody loved him and that he had no purpose in living. When his car engine died, he had gotten out to check under the hood to see if he could find a

Chapter 1 – Embracing Life's Experiences

problem. Finding no problem, he tried again to start the car. It started just as I was pulling in behind him. He went on to say, "When you yelled to me that God loves me, I knew that had to be true. I knew that it must be true because nobody would follow me like you have to tell me that if it were not true." He continued, "Sir, God just used you to spare my life." We wept together.

I never saw or heard from him again, but I am confident that God used that incident to touch a young man's life by letting him know how loved he was by God. The fact is, God also changed my life. I would never be the same! Now I was sure that there was a place for walking in the Spirit or living my life in such a way that God Himself would walk with me. I had the sense that I had caught a glimpse of what many men and women of God before me had experienced. People like King David, Samuel, Moses, Joshua, and those like the Apostle Paul had learned that there is a walk with God that is dynamic. It is possible for us to walk in such a way if we are willing to abandon ourselves to the will of God. Obeying God results in dynamic experiences. Had I not responded to the promptings of God in this situation, the colors of that experience for both the young man and I would have been of a very different hue. He might have taken his life, and I might have missed one of the most important lessons of my life.

Life is an endless journey filled with events, circumstances, people, and decisions that collectively contribute to our character. The influence these experiences have on us reflect

Chapter 1 – Embracing Life's Experiences

the people we have become, our character, and personality conforming to that which we accept as part of life. It is important that we experience God in His fullness. To do so means that we experience His nature and become more like Jesus. To attempt living a godly life without experiencing Him not only is vain but also it will never happen. To attempt such is mere religious activity. Many religionists in Jesus' day thought they could live off the experiences of their ancestors Abraham, Isaac, and Jacob; but with no experience of their own, not only could they not relate to Jesus, they became his antagonists. Many Pharisees never experienced a personal relationship with Jesus. Thus, their experiences kept them from entering the Kingdom of God, because they insisted on embracing a relationship with God that was based on the experiences of their ancestors. Richard E. Simmons III in his book, *The True Measure of a Man* (Evergreen Press, Mobile, AL p.52), made a powerful statement. "In the midst of the storms of life we will either allow what we are experiencing to influence our view of God, or we will allow our view of God to influence what we are experiencing." In other words, we can allow faith to influence what we are experiencing, or we can embrace a distorted view of God.

Do you believe God cares about every aspect of your life? God allows us to have practical, personal contact with Him in this life. A spiritual walk means being involved with, participating in, and obeying of God's will. That's what Jesus came to do. He came to let men experience God in the flesh as Emmanuel, or God with us. God's will is that we experience Him. He lives in us by the Holy Spirit, and as we

Chapter 1 – Embracing Life's Experiences

yield to Him, He becomes more involved in every activity of our lives. Believe that He wants what is best for you and that every good and perfect gift comes from Him. The Scripture says all things work together for good to them that love Him. The "all things" spoken of here include the experiences of your life.

How do we walk in a dynamic way? Here are a few simple steps you may take. These steps are not intended to be used as a formula, nor are they conclusive. What they do represent are measures that I have personally taken, and which have become part of my life experience and testimony. God has no favorites. What He has done for me and others, He will do for you.

Pray
A prayer is a form of communication. Jesus taught us to pray in faith, believing. When you pray, believe. All things are possible to the one who believes. (Mark 9:23; 11:24 KJV)

Listen
God still speaks to us by His Spirit today. Jesus said, "My sheep hear My voice." God speaks in many ways. I address this subject in detail in my new book, but suffice it to say that God wants you to hear His voice. He created you with spiritual ears. We are exhorted to not only be hearers of the Word, but doers as well. If we hear clearly what the Lord is saying to us, we will be prompted to action. (John 10:27; James 1:22-25 KJV)

Chapter 1 – Embracing Life's Experiences

Obey

We used to sing a song with lyrics that said, "Trust and obey, for there's no other way…." Obey the written Word of God and the promptings of God. The promptings will not be contrary to God's written word. They will always be in keeping with His written Word, the Bible, or it is safe to say it is not of God. (I Sam.15:22; I Thessalonians 2:13 KJV)

We can embrace life's experiences with gratitude and thankfulness, realizing that God is keeping His word to make us more like Him. Not to do so means that we, perhaps like the children of Israel, are being stubborn and resistant to God working in us. The forty-year trek in the wilderness serves as a prime example of people who allowed circumstances to overwhelm them. Although the Israelites had experienced God's love, presence and power in delivering them from the oppression of Egypt, they were quick to forget. The circumstances in which they found themselves, sometimes overshadowed God's promises to them. The result was often a less than desirable experience for the Israelites. That is not to condemn them, but rather to point out that we also tend to forget God's love and promises to us. For the Israelites, not embracing God's provision and plan to bring them into the promised land in spite of their circumstances left an entire generation of Israelites to die in the wilderness. The author of Hebrews admonishes us not to fall after the same manner of unbelief, but by faith and grace to enter the promised land. Circumstances will neither empower one to enter God's promises nor prevent one from entering those promises.

Chapter 1 – Embracing Life's Experiences

Time and circumstance happen to all of us, but it is how we respond to God in those circumstances that will determine the quality of our experience.

My prayer for those who read this book is that you experience God in all your circumstances. He has promised to lead you, guide you, and provide for you. Your experiences will become your testimony. In other words, your testimony becomes your unique story. May your story always bring honor and glory to God.

About the Author – Dr. Gary Adams

D.Lit., MA, CMAS

Dr. Gary Adams is an author, contracted public speaker for Mike Rodriguez International, LLC, and a minister. He is the Vice President and Director of Education for the University of Israel Theological Seminary (UITS). He has a passion for educating and training leadership in both corporate and ministry organizations. He has specialized in teaching Bible, Emergency Management and disaster response/recovery both nationally and

Chapter 1 – Embracing Life's Experiences

internationally. He began teaching emergency management from a Christian worldview while a faculty member at Ecclesia College in Springdale, Arkansas. He has been involved for forty-eight years in active ministry, many of those years as a pastor, and in foreign and domestic missions. He has experience in the administration of faith-based agency development and effective execution of humanitarian aid programs. He has experience in disaster relief work and provision of humanitarian assistance throughout the Americas, Mexico, Europe, and Asia. His broad background includes law enforcement and federal disaster assistance. Dr. Adams held press credentials in the 1980's and participated in radio and television talk shows on Central American affairs. He served on the Board of Governors for the American Coalition of Traditional Values (ACTV) with Dr. Tim LaHaye. He is a Senior Consultant in Emergency Management for Alpha Omega Solutions, LLC (AOS), a security consulting company providing solutions for all aspects of global security concerns.

Dr. Adams and Ruth, his lovely wife of 53 years reside in North Central Texas. They have three grown children, fourteen grandchildren, and one great-grandchild.

Contact Dr Gary Adams
GaryAdams@GaryAdamsInternational.com
www.GaryAdamsInternational.com

Chapter 2

The Power of Prayer
By Jillian Murphy

The morning of September 24, 2015, I was driving back from my concurrent classes at the local community college. As a 17-year-old girl, I was behind the wheel of my yellow Volkswagen Beetle. I was driving and just had to go straight ahead for about a quarter of a mile back to my high school for classes. The two lanes suddenly merged into one and the other car did not see how fast it was coming. I can only assume the woman saw a rush of orange cones closing her lane and my rush of yellow to get into the other lane. Well, her choice was to slam right into my car. She hit me and created my very first car accident.

Many can remember their very first car accident, and I will never forget mine. I immediately called my mom. The phone went to voicemail. It was like a rush of everything I had ever learned was spinning around in the car whispering for me to do it, but I couldn't. I couldn't do anything. I tried to pull over to let other cars pass but my head started hurting. Then, one of the whispers finally set in to my mind. Call 911. I called the police and remembered trying to tell them where I was. The tears started to roar from my face. I could barely speak.

Chapter 2 – The Power of Prayer

Then, like a flash, the police were there. They had the woman out of her car talking to them and the two police officers kept looking at me. I was sitting there frozen. I was mortified as to what had just happened, but even more blessed looking over my body that everything was fine.

This reminded me of a story, later on, my mom told me: "When you were a baby girl... I was so blessed and so overjoyed to see you. I took you into my arms, and I started counting your ten little toes and ten little fingers. I wanted to make sure you were all healthy. You were and I cried of joy."

In that moment, I checked myself to see if everything was in place. I was not hurt externally and I just started crying. At this point, the police officers may have guessed that I was younger, because one of the officers came over and asked me to open my door and I did. He looked at me and immediately I knew I was safe. This police officer walked me through the entire process. He asked me for my phone to take pictures of the other car. He took pictures of my car. He asked where I kept my insurance...he took care of everything.

Then, the police officer came back to me and asked me how I was feeling and if I remembered what happened. With streaks of tears, now dried, burning onto my face I croaked that, "I think I am fine. I feel fine. I just want my mommy. All I remember was getting slammed into and my side hitting the middle console." He continued to take care of everything and gave me my phone when he saw my mom calling. I talked to my mom and she was now on her way to meet me at the school. The police officer looked at me and told me, "I know this is a scary time right now, but you will be okay.

Chapter 2 – The Power of Prayer

Do you believe that?" I just nodded my head right back at him. Realizing only then that there was something completely different about him.

I was escorted back to my high school to wait for my mom to pick me up. The police officer took care of everything, calling the policer officer at my school, letting her know that I was in a car accident and will not be attending school today. I was checked out of school as soon as my mom arrived.

When my mom appeared, it was like a whirlwind of emotions hit me. She was crying as I could see in her eyes and her hands were touching me making sure that I was okay. I was alright. She cried and held me and asked me how I felt. I just remember saying I was fine but just wanted to go home. As I got in the car, I told my mom about the police officer and how he took care of everything for me. How I didn't have to lift a hand or anything. My mom looked at me and told me how she is so glad that God sent someone to be there for me to protect me and guide me. I remember pondering on this.

Everything came in like a rush when I was in the Emergency Room. They did scan after scan. In one, I believe it was the CAT scan, a nurse told me that she was sorry for all of the scans and tests they were doing on me, but they just wanted to make sure I was completely healthy. I nodded at her as I tried to show her I understood. She told me that in this scan I would not be able to move for a long time so we could talk if I want. I never remember talking to her. I just remember mentally chewing everything that had just happened. After my wreck, my first call was my mom, who could not be there. But there was this police officer that took care of everything

Chapter 2 – The Power of Prayer

for me. Absolutely everything. I couldn't help but wonder if he was God sent. If this was Christ's touch in the situation. There can always be good found in every situation and as a Christian, we do not see how the rest of the world sees. In Matthew 13:16-17 it says, "But blessed are your eyes, for they see, and your ears, for they hear. For truly, I say to you, many prophets and righteous people longed to see what you see, and did not see it, and to hear what you hear, and did not hear it." This verse pinpoints how as Christians we don't see the world the same. People long to see what we see. We should be able to find Jesus in every situation and because of that, we can see the good in every situation. People long to see the good in everything, but they do not see as we see.

If you have ever worn glasses, you have had this experience on your own. You go throughout your life doing your own thing for such a long time. Then, one day the optometrist tells you that you will be needing glasses. Everything that needs to go into getting a person glasses happens, but then there is the moment when your glasses come in.

When I was little, I remember putting on my glasses and not understanding that I needed them until I had them on. Once I placed the glasses on, it all became clear, literally. I did not know how much I was missing until I placed the glasses on. I remember taking off my glasses and putting them back on multiple times. I would have never known what I was missing. And it was something completely beautiful.

It is the same thing with having spiritual eyes. We do not know how much we are missing until we recognize that all God does is for our good. Then, we can truly place on the

Chapter 2 – The Power of Prayer

spiritual glasses to see out into our lives. Our spiritual glasses will help us see the world as a better place. We will be able to pinpoint light when everyone else can only see darkness. We will be able to find the one flower in the soil that seems barren. We will see the crack of sunlight trying to fight off the darkness. In everything we will see things through the eyes of having our Eternal Father, who loves us with an unconditional love. Sometimes, people never see the difference until they place on their glasses.

I realized through all of my encounters that morning that I needed to focus on the good. The good placed in front of me was the police officer. He was my strength, protection, and helper. He was Christ's touch in the whole situation. One person and one good thing can change a whole situation. Then all of the sudden I had to leave the machine behind and was placed into a room for the doctor to come and talk to my family and me.

Little did I know that the moment between my Savior and me in all of the scans was much needed. All that was in the past was just battle one. The funny thing is, in Christ we already have the victory, but in our life situations we often forget that. With battle one over, I was ready to hear from the doctor and go home. One thing I have learned is you are either exiting a battle, about to go into a battle, or in a battle when it comes to life. And many times we don't even know where we stand.

I was trying to fall asleep and rest, but because they found out that I had a concussion, no one was letting me rest. No one was even letting me sleep. Waiting for the doctor just seemed like the finale of today's show was finally going to come to an end.

Then, the doctor walked in. There was a solace about him. He did not seem sad, but he did not seem happy. My mind rushed back to when I was a freshman in high school and my medical terminology teacher told us how we should approach patients. The lesson was a very long list of "do's and don'ts," but the main idea of the lesson that I pulled was: do not scare the patients with what you know and do not let them read anything from your face, it will worry them. Looking at this doctor, I felt like we were having the same thought process because his face wasn't happy or sad. Finally, he told us "I have good news and bad news for you all today. The good news is Ms. Jillian did not obtain any serious injuries. From the wreck, she has a minor concussion, but besides that, she is healthy." I was overjoyed to hear those words. Now, I can go home. Looking back at the doctor I forgot… he had bad news as well. He continued on to say, "We did find a prior existing condition. Jillian…" The doctor seemed to talk in slow motion. Nothing was moving fast enough. I thought I was healthy. Thought? I am healthy. There is nothing wrong with me at all. I am fine. I had to slowly settle down my brain to hear what he was trying to tell me, but I missed it. Everyone's eyes in the room went to me and looked so hurt and worried. I looked into my mom's eyes and it was like she was trying to fend off the tears. I looked back at the doctor, and I think he understood that I had no idea what was going on.

Chapter 2 – The Power of Prayer

He then said "You have two tumors, one on each ovary. The one on the right side is the size of a grapefruit and if you lay back, you can feel it yourself. The other on the left, is the size of a lemon." He continued to talk about how he was not a specialist in this area and could not tell us anymore than that. We would need to talk to a specialist.

Well, I was sitting there and my world froze. Two tumors? Why is everyone still talking and saying things? I have two tumors. What does this mean… I don't understand… All of these thoughts were swirling around in my mind and I was just so tired. I believe now that I was also spiritually tired. I had just left one battle to walk straight into the next and this is how it is sometimes in life. In 1 Peter 5:6-7 it says "Humble yourselves, therefore, under the mighty hand of God so that at the proper time he may exalt you, casting all your anxieties on him, because he cares for you." In this moment, I knew I was too tired to deal with this on my own. Also, I reminded myself of all I have learned, my burden is never meant to be carried on my own. I am called to give my burdens and anxieties to the Lord. I tried to focus on this as my world kept spinning.

My heart sunk into the pit of my stomach. The room seemed to evaporate away. Somehow, in the midst of the chaos of this news, I just started to question everything. "Why was I put on this earth just to possibly have cancer my senior year of high school? What is the point of living if I still believe I have so much more to do?" I thought of the people who were diagnosed with cancer in my life and how kind and sweet they are. I became so angry. I could feel myself fuming from the inside. How? How could these people, diagnosed with cancer, be so thankful for each day they live knowing that the next one isn't promised? In James 4:13-15 it says, "Come now, you who say, 'Today or tomorrow we will go into such and such a town and spend a year there and trade and make a profit' yet you do not know what tomorrow will bring. What is your life? For you are a mist that appears for a little time and then vanishes. Instead, you ought to say, 'If the Lord wills, we will live and do this or that.'" I knew what the bible said about each day not being promised. I knew that we are like a mist that vanishes in time, but there is always a difference between hearing it and living it. In this moment, I was living it. I started to look over to my mom, who seemed to be trying to hold it all together. But in the midst of all this support, I felt alone. I was now carrying what seemed to be an immeasurable burden.

The doctor continued to tell us how he was not a specialist. He could not tell me anything about the tumor, my health, or anything regarding it except that it was there. He said that we would have to make an appointment with a specialist, then they would refer us to a surgeon. He wished us best of luck. While walking out I felt as if every eye was on me, waiting for me to crumble. But I was fuming on the inside, the pain and tears had not set in. As we left, my mom looked over to me and told me that tonight would be a good night to go watch the movie *War Room*.

The Christian movie had been in theaters for a little while now and we were hearing all of the great reviews over it, but never had the time. My mom advised me, which was wise

Chapter 2 – The Power of Prayer

council, to cling to the Lord in this time and to try not to become upset over what could be when we do not know. This is so true and in the midst of many battles in our life, we need people that will always direct us back to the Lord. Because at the end of the day many people may think they can give sound advice or may think they know how to solve a problem you are in, but nobody knows the future but the Lord. No one knows the plans ahead but God. In this situation, I learned to seek the Lord.

The ride to the movie theater seemed to blur, but I remember the thoughts rushing over me. I kept thinking of my purpose and how I was trying to bargain with God and tell Him that I have so much to offer and not to let me go. I was pleading with the Lord for it not to be my time. The tears slowly started to roll down my cheeks as I knew that I had no control over what was going to happen and what I was going to find out. Everything is in the Lord's hands and I have to be able to trust in Him and allow His plan to work. I knew all of the right things… I was taught all of the right things. But in the situation, none of them felt right. None of them felt near and dear to my heart. They all seemed like fact less clichés rolling off the tongues of people who didn't understand.

As we walked into the movie theater, my heart felt like it was callousing over. I did not want to watch a Christian movie and hear how great God is all the time. I wanted a specialist appointment. I wanted to know my health. I wanted to know the future now. I did not know that this movie was going to be one of the main things that helped me through the fear of the unknown.

The movie spoke to the trials in our lives and how we are going through a war in life. Satan is constantly asking God for permission to tempt us and give us trials. Then, the movie focused on the power of prayer, how for Christians, our prayer is our fight and the prayer room was the war room. My huge take away from the movie was how we need to fight for everything in our lives. We need to fight through prayer and let God do the rest. In this, we need to understand that prayer is not a passive action to be taken, but is an active fight and stance in our relationship with Christ. God hears each prayer, each plea, each cry out to Him. He knows what we are going through and even more than that, He knows why we are going through it. So, if we lean upon Him, He will surely lead us out of the storm.

I sat at the end of the movie, in tears. Silent tears. They quietly stretched down my face. I couldn't believe that this movie was the exact encouragement I needed. It convicted me in how I was doubting already my relationship with Christ and how powerful my God was. I knew I needed to step back and ask myself the question. Jillian… How big is your God? The answer I knew, but earlier was buried beneath the anger, fear, and hurt. My God is all-powerful, He is a mighty Savior, He is a provider, protector, healer, and He is the Great I Am. So why would I live in fear? There has never been a moment that has surprised the Lord and I knew now that this was somewhere in His plan.

Chapter 2 – The Power of Prayer

The first office visit to the specialist finally came. The wonder of everything I would find out was a cloud following me everywhere. I couldn't tell my small group at church or anyone because the thought of saying it out loud just made it a little more real and I did not want any of this nightmare to become real. Walking into the office, the elephant in the room became even more prominent. I walked into the four white walls that seemed to be holding the answer to a question that was holding my life in the balance. The specialist was very kind. She told us that she looked over the scans. She tried to explain all of these medical terms and all of the possibilities of how these two tumors may have formed. At the end of the day, I was just waiting for my clean bill of health.

Then, she addressed me. "Do you want kids?" What kind of question is this, I thought to myself. Out loud I responded "Yes, I would love to have kids in the future." Then, it hit me and I couldn't believe it did not hit me before. You need ovaries to have children. The tumors are on both of my ovaries. I do not even have one healthy ovary. She then went on to explain she could not tell us if it was cancer or not, but the tumors needed to be taken out immediately. The one on the right, which was a size of a grapefruit, was so large that if anything would happen to it, that it may move, then it could do serious damage. She said it was a blessing that the tumor did not move during my car accident, and it was even more of a blessing that we found the tumors through the car accident, because I would have never even known.

Chapter 2 – The Power of Prayer

Still, she continued on to tell me how there were various possibilities on how to take out the tumors. She did inform me that I might not be able to keep both of my ovaries, because of the size of the tumors, but she knows the surgeon will try. The pain sunk in more than ever. I might not be able to have kids.

She asked me if I wanted to have kids to see the importance of my ovaries to me. She asked me these questions to form a method to save my ovaries. All of this started to pile into my brain and I realized that I may never get to have a child. I may never get to have the blessing of giving birth to my child and seeing what a wonderful blessing it can be. Immediately I thought of the bible story of Sarai and Abram in Genesis 16 of how she had Abram sleep with her female servant because she could not have a child. This story always seemed silly to me. Like why would you let your husband sleep with another woman, just to have a child? Then, the Lord pointed out how little her faith was because she took the situation into her own hands instead of waiting for God's divine plan. Then, she was able to have a child, but she created a mess. She made her bed and now she had to lay in it.

I always thought Sarai acted way too prematurely. Like you want to go back in time and ask her, "Why couldn't you just see God's plan? Why couldn't you just be still and know that everything will work out for the glory of Christ?" But how many times do we do this in our own lives? I never thought I would want to prematurely jump before God's plan for my life. I never thought I would try to take my life into my own

Chapter 2 – The Power of Prayer

hands instead of trying to obediently listen to God's will, until this moment in the doctor's office. It all suddenly clicked in my mind. Sarai could not see how it was possible in her own eyes, so she thought she had to take control. In this moment in my life, I was wondering why I hadn't taken control of my life. I was back to my doubt that God had just delivered me from.

I started to contemplate how I could have gone outside of God's plan. I could have gotten pregnant and been a teenage mother, which to the world, may seem awful, but at least I would be able to have a child. At least I would be able to have a son or daughter to call my own. I didn't hear anything else that office visit. All of it went in one ear and out the other. All I could mentally chew on was the possibility of never having kids.

The next day when I got out of classes, I had to pick up my "nanny children." Waiting in the carpool lane, I just started to bawl and I cried out to God asking Him, "Why? Why would you take this from me? Why would you put the burden of not having children and possibly having cancer on me? I am the person who looks at children and sees the beauty in each smile and laugh. I love children. I want to be a mother, Lord. Please, do not take this from me. Please do not steal this from me. I need to have children. I need to." As I wiped away my tears, the kids got into the car, and I drove to their house. We talked about their day and I helped them with homework, all while still looking at them and wondering if I will ever get to do this with my own children. Will I ever get to see my child want to play on the trampoline instead of doing addition? Or need help coloring in a poster for a project due the next day? Will I even get to live to my high school graduation or will you take me beforehand?

All of these questions started to consume me. The questions not only started to consume me but also started to consume my life. Sadly, I started distancing myself from the Lord. I did not read my bible every day. In church services, I would sit and listen, but I would not want to learn anything from it. I didn't want to take anything away. I wanted to come and sit and leave the exact same way because that was something I could control in my life, whether I chose to listen or not. I stopped pursuing everything. I did not want to go to club meetings and I did not want to apply to do anything. God blessed me with early acceptance to a lot of schools because if not I don't believe I would have been able to apply anywhere. I drowned myself into a state of self-loathing. I did not want to be happy and I did not want to see a light at the end of the tunnel. I did not want to smile or laugh. I wanted to know. I wanted this nightmare to be over. I wanted this not to be real, but it was all too real.

One Sunday, my small group leader talked to me. She pointed out that I had been very distant and asked if I had anything on my heart. At this point, I realized that I was letting Satan rule my life. I was allowing my situation to determine my mood and the way I acted, when my character and the way I live for Christ should never ever depend on situations. Situations change like a gust of the wind, but a foundation in Christ is something I can stand firm upon. I allowed myself to do the thing that I was fearing for so long,

Chapter 2 – The Power of Prayer

I allowed myself to make my situation to become more real and tell my small group.

I told them and they all surrounded me as I cried because I knew it was no longer just my battle, but they will be fighting with me as well. My small group and my small group leader began to pray over me and something happened. Some of the weight of the burden I was carrying was lifted. I no longer had to fight this fight on my own but with prayer warriors in my small group by my side.

I realized that it was a ploy of Satan to keep me isolated all along. Isolated, he knew that I would dwell on my thoughts and be lost in my own self-pity. With fellow Christians by my side, Satan knew that I would become strong in the body of Christ because now they are praying with me and alongside me. Now that my struggle was brought into the light I was able to move forward.

Allowing my small group to know made me realize that I took a step in the right direction, but I was far from being okay. The next day when I went back into my quiet time after a long time away, the Lord spoke to me. I knew He was asking me, "My child, why are you running? Why are you angry?" This question kept tossing around in my mind. I kept denying it, that I'm no longer running from the Lord. I might have been at first when I just found out. But God, look at me now. I told my table group and they are praying for me. I opened up my bible today. I am not running and I am not angry. Well, not angry at my God, but angry with the situation. Today, I can spot my denial from a mile away, whereas then, I truly tried to convince myself of this fact.

Chapter 2 – The Power of Prayer

Later on that week, we had a worship session for my student ministry at my church. I went in with the intention of singing worship songs, all of the feel good easy Christian things that I thought I could gloss over. The truth was, with the first song the Lord penetrated my heart. I felt a conviction of how fake I was being and the questions again came into my mind. I knew I needed to be honest with myself. I was told over and over in my mind to be truthful. The worship leader and everyone around me started to sing, "You are good, you are good." Finally, my lips sealed shut. My eyes began to water and I knew I could not allow myself to sing that lie. I recognized I was angry with God. The God that saved me. The God who I knew how great and powerful He is. I was angry with Him. I hated myself for being so angry with my Savior. I knew that I was running from God. Deep down in my heart, I thought, just maybe, if I run far enough away from God, He will change His mind. He will change what is in store for me because He knows I am not strong enough to handle it.

I walked away from the worship service towards the back, with every intention of leaving. I ran straight into my girl's minister. She held me close and I just let all my tears out. I didn't know I could have any more left. After I got it all out I told her that I was worried and I was angry. I didn't want to have cancer. I wanted children more than I have ever wanted anything else. I didn't want this to be the end. I want to graduate. I want to get married one day. I have so many things that I still want to do. And with a lump forming in my throat I asked, "What if I don't get to do any of these things?" I remember she reminded me to look toward Christ.

Chapter 2 – The Power of Prayer

I need to stand on my rock that is Christ Jesus. He knew each day I was going to live even before I was born. He knows the plan. Then, she challenged me and asked me, "Is our Lord good?" At the time, I laughed a little and said of course. And then she prayed over me. She also asked if she could come to the surgery and I told her she could.

Walking away from her, I went over to the wall and sunk to the floor. What kind of question is it...Is the Lord good? Of course He is good! Why wouldn't God be good? Of course my Savior is powerful. Then, I had a rush all over my body and I remember sitting there in the midst of everyone worshipping and I realized everything she wanted me to see and what Christ was bringing to my heart. Despite the situation, God is good. As a little girl, I remember hearing all of these church folks coming in and saying "God is good" and the next person would respond back, "All the time, He is good." The saying seems so mindless. But it became real to me.

I bowed my head and everything else faded away. I prayed in a way I never have before. I just talked to my Lord, and it was the most bare and raw prayer I have ever had. I just whispered… "Jesus, Jesus, Jesus. Please save me. Please save me from this anger that has consumed me. Lord I am sorry I doubted your power. I am sorry I would ever try and turn from you. Lord, I dare ask that you let me be healthy and I get to have kids. BUT God I know… if not, you are still good. Jesus, if I have cancer, you are good. If I am healthy, you are good. If I am never able to have kids, you are good. If I am able to have kids, you are good. If none of this is in your plan, you are good. No matter my situation, you are good and I know that now." When I raised my head from that prayer, ALL of the burden was lifted from me. Everything was shifted from me carrying the weight of the world onto my powerful Savior carrying the weight for me and that is exactly how it was intended to be.

When I got up off the ground, the pastor was making an announcement to go and write on a piece of red paper who God is to us. Then, one of the last songs of the night came on. The words stopped me in my tracks. I listened carefully. Everyone sang around me, "You split the sea so I could walk right through it." I knew the analogy was to Moses and the going across the Red Sea. This analogy became my saying from that point on. The song wasn't only addressing biblical times of how the Lord helped Moses and the Israelites across the Red Sea. The song was also referring to how the Lord will always have a pathway through every trial we may be facing. Even when we can see no way out, our God can do the impossible.

Moses must have been looking at that sea and asking himself how he got there and why the Lord would take them that far just to fail then. With more trouble with the pharaoh and his men on the way, the pressure upon Moses and his faith must have been immense. Moses turned to God. Where Moses and no one else saw a way, God created a way by splitting the Red Sea. God split the sea so they could walk right through it. Realizing all of this, I decided I knew exactly which word I would write onto my card.

Chapter 2 – The Power of Prayer

I walked right over to the station, picked up a red card and wrote down the boldest word that I believed my God is. I wrote "Healer." At the time, I did not know what my future held, but I knew that God knew. And I believed that He could heal me. I folded the red piece of paper into my wallet and kept it there, to be reminded at any time that I began to doubt God that God was my Healer.

The day of surgery came and my heart was beating out of my chest. I knew that it was in God's hands, but I thought, "Today is the day. Today is the day that will shape my life, that will allow me to see what God has in store for me. I will learn my purpose through this situation." As I walked into a massive hospital, my hand clung to my mother's, holding on tightly.

We got through all of the pre-operational details and they told me I could wait in the waiting room because there was a party waiting for me. When I walked into the room, there were many people waiting, possibly for someone to get out of surgery or to go in. Then, I spotted my student ministry's staff. They came over to me and told me how they have been waiting for me and how they have been praying for me. They were all smiling and had such a light coming through them that I felt a hope in the presence of other Christians. This hope was of their prayers and of the faith we all had together that our God can do the impossible. As they started to pray over me, I felt safe. I felt the protective power of my Almighty God rushing over me. In that moment, I did not hold any fear and knew exactly that everything was in His hands. After the prayer, one of the ministers came up to me and gave me a little cross and inside was a poem. The title of the poem was "A Cross in My Pocket." The poem shared that this was a cross to carry with me to know that the Lord's presence is with me. I found a peace in it, not in the material of the cross, but of what it represented. The cross represented that even in this immeasurable trial standing before me, the Lord has everything in control and will walk with me through it. Deuteronomy 31:6 came to mind "Be strong and courageous. Do not fear or be in dread of them, for it is the Lord your God who goes with you. He will not leave you or forsake you." I found such a peace with that verse in the back of my mind and rubbing my fingers over this small cross. My youth minister told me that this little elderly lady in the corner made it and was handing it to people before they went into surgery. I went over to her and told her that I was going into surgery today and thank you for reminding me of how great our God is. She told me she would pray for me. That little elderly lady, along with countless prayers, helped to lift me up to the Lord before I went into my battle.

Before going into surgery, I felt at peace. I knew that no matter the outcome that the Lord was still good. I reminded myself that my God is so much bigger than my circumstances. I looked over to my mom and she prayed over me a final time. The whole prayer of the innermost part of my heart was still praying for a miracle. I didn't want to speak it out loud because I knew I had full faith in the Lord's plan being greater than my own. I looked over to my mom after the prayer and asked her, "What if they take my ovaries?" Then, she looked at me with her eyes turning glassy

Chapter 2 – The Power of Prayer

like tears were about to fall and she explained to me, "Jilli...they will have to call out to me before they take out either of your ovaries, but I will let you know the outcome right when you get out of surgery hunny." That was the final reassurance I needed. It seems silly to find reassurance in the fact that they will have to ask my mom before they take out either of my ovaries, but I have faith that my mom knows exactly what to do.

The anesthesiologist gave me anesthesia and I soon was completely knocked out, fully dependent on the Lord.

Before that day, I had never had surgery, ever. When I woke up it felt like I was watching a movie with the dramatic effects of everything being blurred because the character was in a dream. In the midst of the blur, I woke up to see my small group leader bringing in my favorite chocolate shake from Chick-fil-A and my friends and family surrounding me. I couldn't remember much, but realized that they were there and that I was out of surgery. I looked over to my left and my mom was by my side holding and rubbing her thumb over my hand.

I guess I slipped out of consciousness because when I woke back up again there were no people, just my mom and me. I looked over to her and through my lips I croaked "Like sunlight burning at midnight, making my life something so beautiful, beautiful." Words to a song that we had been listening to on the ride up to surgery. She carefully started to sing with me. She seemed to read my mind as I croaked the words. She leaned over and whispered in my ear, "I get to be a grandma one day." Tears started to flow from my face, as

Chapter 2 – The Power of Prayer

I realized I was still able to have kids. The song "Beautiful, Beautiful" was so true. How in the midst of the darkest of times, God's light can still shine through. I slipped back to sleep.

When I woke up again, I was being admitted to stay overnight. My mom was still by my side. As we were placed in my room for the night, she explained to me the logistics of my surgery. She told me that when they went into my right ovary and tried to remove the tumor, the tumor was too large. This tumor was the size of a grapefruit and there was no way to save my ovary. They called out to my mom and she gave permission that they could take it. She then told me, that we went over to my left ovary to take out the tumor the size of a lemon. When they went to take out the tumor, they were faced with a completely healthy ovary. The tumor was gone…

A warmth filled all over my body and all I could say is "God is good." I kept repeating that to myself over and over again that God is good. I was overwhelmed with emotions and could not help but to praise my God. I looked over to my mom as she continued to tell me that I can have children in the future with one ovary. She explained that they do have to biopsy the tumor they did remove and let us know the result at my post-surgery appointment.

My heart was so full…the Lord took away the tumor. The Lord made the impossible, possible. He is such a mighty God. I could never have even prayed or imagined that the tumors or even one of the tumors to just disappear. But He knew His plan, He knew exactly the plan for my life. God is

Chapter 2 – The Power of Prayer

so good. I could not stop praising the Lord and I just laid in my hospital room in awe of the power of my Savior. I have heard and read about miracles, but I never could have ever imagined that the Lord would work one right within me.

I was on cloud nine after my surgery. I knew we did not know the results of the biopsy yet, but there is something about after God performing the impossible, there are no restrictions on what the Lord can do in my life or anyone else's. We did get the call that the results were in and had to drive up to the surgeon's office.

There was a different feel walking into his office this time. Waiting in the waiting room wasn't an anticipation if God will provide or what God's plans will be. This time waiting, I was positive that God was my Healer, my Provider, my Protector and I couldn't be more thankful. Walking in to get my check up, I felt like I was walking on air. Where there was pain and insecurity before, there was confidence in the power of my Savior. The surgeon walked in and he immediately started to ask me how I felt. I told him that I felt great!

Then the conversation shifted to the results of the biopsy. He told me that my biopsy report was very short and that is something to be very thankful for in my case. He called me in to check on me and to let me know that the tumor was benign. I did not have cancer. I did not know my heart could become even more full than before, but it did. The surgeon then went on to explain how he did not know how my tumor on the left could have disappeared. He started to kind of ramble off to himself, maybe to come up with a scientific explanation of how a tumor could be so obviously there and then gone when it comes to the day for it to be removed. I looked at him before he could even say anything and said, "It is a miracle, I serve a great God." He looked at me and did not say anything but smiled and nodded. He continued to talk to my mom about various, different technical details of how I should be feeling, when I could dance again, etc. The surgeon then gave me his card and told me that I could call him if I needed anything or if I experienced any certain type of pain. I told him thank you.

Walking out of the office, I just looked up at the bright blue sky and whispered, "Thank you." I knew that there was no scientific explanation and there was no way someone could deny the power of my Savior. On the way back home, I sat in the car re-playing my past few months back in my mind. I got into a car accident that caused us to find the tumors in the first place. Then, time after time God sent people to encourage me which allowed me to know that He is with me and He has a greater purpose, all the way to this moment where I still have one healthy left ovary and how I will still be able to have children and do not have cancer. I never felt so alive. God proved himself to me and I could never deny His wonderful presence.

God proves His presence to us all the time. In our everyday lives, God proves His unconditional love for us. If we choose to put on our spiritual glasses and choose to see Him, a lot of the questions we have will be answered. In all of the unknowns, we will be able to find peace in the midst of it all because of our God, who is the Great I Am.

Chapter 2 – The Power of Prayer

With our confidence in our Lord and Savior, we will follow His purpose for our lives through faith and persistent prayer.

If you would like to read more about how to see God's hand and finding God's *why* in the midst of our trials, read Jillian's new book, *"This is Why"* releasing in June 2017.

About the Author – Jillian Murphy

Jillian Murphy started her freshman year at a Christian university in Oklahoma, pursuing a degree in nursing in 2016. Jillian felt her call to ministry the Summer of 2014 on a mission trip in Washington D.C. She followed God's plan for her life by interning at a women's safe house in Dallas, TX, Restored Hope Ministries, starting in the Fall of 2014. Jillian published her first book "The Four Seasons of Hope" July 2016. She wrote this book while she was still in high school. She continues to have a passion to use her writing to proclaim God's name. Jillian has fallen in love with speaking to women. She talks about the seasons of life we are in as Christians and the why behind our difficult circumstances. She encourages people to live a life that will convince others to follow Christ. She is thankful for all God has done in her life and prays that she will continue to follow God's will in the future. Jillian's goal

Chapter 2 – The Power of Prayer

is to pursue writing more books, speaking to people about Jesus, and to impact lives in the name of Jesus. Stay tuned for Jillian's journey!

Contact Jillian Murphy:

www.JillianMurphy.org

Chapter 3

The Gift in You
By Mark A. Hernandez

"When you discover your gift, you become a gift to us all"
Mark A. Hernandez

Do you like to receive gifts? If you're like me, you love to receive gifts. Reflect with me when you were a child during Christmas and all you would think about was, "What am I getting for Christmas?" You would look, size-up your gifts, feel them, and shake them up (that's cheating, by the way, which I'm guilty of). Once you're done cheating, your mind would begin to create a picture of possibilities and your mind shifted from "What am I getting?" to "What am I am opening on Christmas day?" The day finally comes with your family and you begin to open your gifts with anticipation and bated breath to finally see what gifts you received. With each unwrapping of your gift, your heartbeat and breathing would get faster and faster. You finally get through all the tape and wrapping paper and with a huge smile on your face and satisfaction you say, "Yes, I got what I wanted!"

Chapter 3 – The Gift in You

Have you ever felt like that, opening a gift that you were so amazed, surprised, and satisfied about that you said, "Yes, this is what I wanted"?

At birth, you and I were given a name and a gift. You are so special (Yes, you!) to God that he gave you a gift that is so amazing and special that he desires for you to discover it and be so surprised that you say "Yes" to it. Remember, just like a child, you must receive your gift and open it in order for it to be a gift. In *1 Peter 4:10 (New Living Translation)* the Bible declares, *"God has given each of you a gift from his great variety of spiritual gifts. Use them well to serve one another."* For those who may say, "I do not have a gift," or "I don't know what my gift is," the bible is very clear in that if you have received Christ as your Lord and Savior, you have a gift. All is not reserved for the high echelon of society, the learned, or the aristocrats, no, ALL is ALL (you and me). Please take a moment to read this verse again and insert your name, then allow the word through the power of the Holy Spirit to fill you with the wonder of what can be amazing and so surprising, through you offering your gift to humanity for the kingdom. Remember, our gifts are not gifts until we receive it, open it, and share it to the world, and then we are using it to serve others as a gift to humanity. It is at this point when we are actually saying, "Yes, this is what I wanted." At the same time, your Heavenly Father looks down from heaven and with such amazement and wonder of who you are and what you will be doing through using your gift and the lives you will be transforming, he says just like any proud father, "Wow, look at what my son/daughter is doing, I'm so proud of them."

Chapter 3 – The Gift in You

Have you have ever lost or misplaced a gift that you received and spent countless hours looking for your it? Then you finally said, "I can't find it" or "I lost it." Sometimes you may not even realize that you lost your gift because you have not used it in such a long time until a condition or circumstance brings to your awareness that you have a gift and you begin to search for it. Think about it like this: when you were a child and received a gift that you had an expectation for, wanted, and valued, you either kept it in a known place or kept it on your person because it was very valuable to you. On the other hand, when you receive a gift that you did not have an expectation for or did not see the value in, you don't even remember where you placed it the second day you received it. Like the Christmas sweater that you opened and said, "Oh, thank you," not, "Yes, this is what I wanted!" The biggest difference I see is the value you place on the gift. The valued gift is one you kept close to you and you knew where it was at all times.

A valued gift I treasure is my grandfather's hat he used to wear; I treasure it for who the gift belonged to and because my mom gave me his hat. For those of you who say, "You know what Mark, I'm not really sure what my gift is," or "I just don't live life with any amazement or enthusiasm anymore," first off, you're not alone. I want to share my personal story with you about how I felt lost because I did not know what my gift was. I no longer saw any potential in myself until the day I was challenged. I firmly believe that if it were not for God intervening through a co-worker and challenging me through a powerful life-changing question,

Chapter 3 – The Gift in You

my life and family's life would be significantly different. That's the power of the gift in you; it will change the trajectory of your life.

Have you have ever heard of scaffold builders or know what a scaffold is? Please take my word and experience, it is hard, physical work. I started out my construction career as a scaffold builder and did not know anything about the craft or trade. A scaffold is a temporary work platform designed to support people, tools, and equipment. Whether you're erecting, dismantling, or modifying a scaffold, it is physical work. Let me give a big shout out to all the scaffold builders – You rock! If it was not for your hard work and craftsmanship, much of the work that needs to be completed would not be.

There is a Hispanic term given to a person from the workers called "Maestro," which means "craftsman." The "Maestro" has knowledge, training, experience, as well as a tremendous amount of influence, trust, and respect from his/her fellow peers. The "Maestro" is usually older and can be seen as a mentor who adds tremendous value to the workforce and the organization by imparting a wealth of knowledge, training, and experience to the next generation of workers. What is interesting is that the term is very different from that of "Jefe," or boss. The key difference is that "Jefe" is given by the employer and "Maestro" is given by the workers. I've been to Mexico, Guatemala, and Paraguay, where the term "Maestro" is used in the same context in each country and the person has the same attributes and qualities that the workers are looking for.

Chapter 3 – The Gift in You

After a couple of years working in the scaffold industry, a man who would become my mentor came beside me. He showed me all the tricks of the trade with scaffold building. He was my "Maestro." My mentor was a tall, light-skinned, hazel green-eyed man who was in his mid-fifties, but could out-work and out-skill many of the younger workers. I loved how he called me "Marcitos." Marcitos is a term of endearment used by a father to his son. I looked up to and had tremendous respect for him and truly saw him as a Mentor. One day during lunch, he asked me in Spanish, "Marcitos, ¿qué estas haciendo aquí?" – "What are you doing here?" The question went right over my head and I told him we're having lunch and to please pass the salsa. You have to understand that like the good Hispanics we are, when we have lunch we put everything in the middle and we all share. He leaned over to me and asked the same question again, "Marcitos, ¿qué estás haciendo aquí?" I gave the same response from the first time, that we're having lunch. I love, love what he did next, it's like the coach wanting to see the athlete cross the goal line. He asked again. This time leaning over, he was right in my face, and as I stared into his hazel-green eyes he asked a series of questions in Spanish. "Mark, you were born in the US?" I replied, "Yes." He asked his second question, "You know how to speak and write English?" I replied, "Yes." He asked his third question, "Marcitos, you graduated high school and went into the military?" I replied, "Yes." He leaned in closer as he asked his final life-changing question, "Marcitos, ¿qué estás haciendo aquí, este trabajo es para el burro?" Translation – "Mark, what are you doing here? This job is for the donkey."

Chapter 3 – The Gift in You

Wow, I was so angry, but I listened. You see, he saw in me what I no longer saw in myself. He saw the gift, he saw more; He saw what could be so amazing and so surprising for others through my gift.

Throughout the day, I had a knot in my gut and later that night I cried like a baby because I began to say to myself, "What am I doing here?" Have you ever been told something that is so true that it shakes you to the core and you do something different? As the saying goes, "Truth hurts." I was angry because I knew what my mentor was saying was true. I did not want to become angry with him because of the investment he made by pouring years of experience into my life, showing his sincere desire to see me grow. Companies invest millions into training their workers annually. There is no dollar amount that can be placed on the investment he gave me and the powerful, challenging question he made that one day during lunch. He gave me the gift of 15 years of experience and the gift of truth in love which changed the trajectory of my life all because he saw value and potential in me. I am forever grateful, Gracias my dear mentor.

If you're reading this, it is because you want to be more, have more, and give more. Many of you may say that you know what your gift is. Others of you may say you don't know what your gift is. My question to you is, are you living a true expression of your gift to the world? I ask you so that you see the gift that you are to us all and so you can become that gift to us all. The world needs your contribution, commitment, courage, compassion, and competence.

Chapter 3 – The Gift in You

The world needs ALL of you, not part of you. The world desperately needs your gift. Discover your gift, work out your gift, and begin today to multiply your gift.

I have a special request for you to demonstrate honor to your Mentor: Please reach out to your "Maestro." Call him or her and tell them 'thank you' for investing in you as well as take them to lunch or dinner. While you're eating, let them know the amazing impact their investment had in your life, let them know that you are forever grateful for them, and that they are a blessing to you and your family. When my son got married, I reached out to my mentors and invited them first, had a special table for them, and let them feel really special. I did not know it then, but after growing in the word of God and studying leadership development and coaching, I understand now my mentor, being a "Maestro" to me all those years and giving me truth one day during lunch, was his gift to me.

Let's go back for a second to what I shared what is an important aspect of the gift: You have to receive it and value it. I could have rejected my mentor's truth, but I was able to receive the gift because I valued it and the giver. Over 20 years later, every time I share this powerful story, I get choked up because I did not realize how powerful of an impact that coaching session had on my life. I had said many times to my wife that if it was not for my mentor, my tools and our family's life would be so dramatically different. All the opportunities, all the blessings, and all the rich experiences would never be known or experienced. Even as

Chapter 3 – The Gift in You

I write these words to you right now, I am reflecting on my three sons whose lives would be so different because my gift would have never manifested and they would never see the dad they know now. The amazing opportunities and blessings God gave me as a result of discovering my gift, working out my gift, and sharing my gift to the world would have never been experienced. I am forever grateful to my mentor for not only asking me a powerful question, but for being like a coach and staying with the process to see the gift come out. Please hear me when I tell you that if God can take a guy from scaffold builder to motivational speaker, God can do the same for you.

I discovered Proverbs 18:16 when I launched my leadership development company. *"A man's gift makes room for him and brings him before great men."* (New American) Your gift WILL, not maybe, make a way. As a result of my mentor's challenge question of 'what am I doing here,' I have discovered my gift, used my gift, and multiplied my gift by the power of the Holy Spirit.

I am the 1st Hernandez to:
- attend college.
- work for the US Department of Labor – OSHA for 12 years.
- launch a leadership development company.
- to become an author.
- go to the John Maxwell team to train leaders in Guatemala and Paraguay.

Also, "My We Is The Key" keynote has reached over 6,000 people.

Chapter 3 – The Gift in You

I do not share these things to impress you. I share them to impress upon you how important your Heavenly Father values you and your gift. Your Heavenly Father honors one thing and one thing only: faith.

It takes faith to receive something you don't see. It takes faith to work something out when you don't see immediate results. It takes faith to multiply your gift, not knowing if there will be a return. Your Heavenly Father honors you and your gift so much that He left an amazing story of a little boy in the New Testament who had a lunch with fish and bread in the midst of thousands of people. Jesus went out among them and found the boy (Your Heavenly Father knows where you are) and asked the boy for his lunch. The boy gave his lunch to Jesus, (if he was Hispanic and had tacos, I'm not so sure) Jesus prayed over the lunch, (blessed it – this is where multiplication occurred) and an amazing thing happened – the boy's lunch fed the thousands of people with enough for leftovers.

This powerful story tells us that the boy had a lunch (his gift), there was a need, the boy gave his gift back to Jesus to be blessed, and multiplication occurred. Why is this story so amazing, you ask? Your Heavenly Father honored the boy so much that this story is shared throughout the gospels.

Discover your gift, use your gift, and multiply your gift, and your Heavenly Father will honor you as well. I am living testimony on this powerful principle, so much so that I decided to call my leadership development company *Multiply Leadership Solutions*.

Chapter 3 – The Gift in You

Everything I do now, I see as a ministry and as exercising my gift in order to expand the kingdom of God. What is so amazing is that God is so faithful in opening doors of opportunity for me and my family. In the process, I have grown spiritually and have a love for personal growth that sharpens my gift of public speaking.

It has been said that people would rather die than be a public speaker. I remember how I was so nervous when I started, and now I get excited about sharing my gift to people and creating a memorable experience for the audience. There have been many times while speaking that my gift takes over and I don't even remember what I said. People come afterwards and say, "I needed to hear that," or "You're so energetic," or "Are you a pastor?" I love the feedback, but I give all the glory to God, for without Him I would not have the gift. Remember, there is no passion in playing small and the world desperately needs your gift. Just like in the story of the boy and his lunch, your gift will be able to meet thousands of people's needs (yes, you). Let that sink in for a moment and tell yourself, "My gift will meet thousands of needs." Think for just a second of the lives that will be transformed like how mine was through the power of being a gift. Think of the stories that will be shared for generations because your gift changed the trajectory of a person's life. Only when we get to heaven will we know, so begin today and remind yourself daily, "I am a walking gift to all those around me." Get ready, get ready, get ready.

Chapter 3 – The Gift in You

Reflection:
Pray for your Gift: Matthew 7: 7-12: Ask, Seek, & Knock: "Ask and it will be given to you; seek and you will find; knock and the door will be opened to you. For everyone who asks receives; the one who seeks finds; and to the one who knocks, the door will be opened."

Ask God, "What is the gift you have for me so that I can be a gift to humanity?" The key is to keep asking, keep seeking, and keep knocking. You may discover, like me, what ends up being a gift you would have never thought you could do or do well. Remember, our responsibility is to receive the gift, value the gift, and value the giver of the gift.

Use Your Gift: Once you discover what you gift is, work at it. You will discover that the more you use your gift, the more opportunities will come up to be a gift to others. The only opportunities that come are the ones you knock on and as a result, God will open more doors so that your gift can be used for his glory. **1 Peter 4:10** God has given each of you a gift from his variety of spiritual gifts. Use them well to serve one another.

Multiply Your Gift: 2 Timothy 2:2 (New American): "The things you have heard from me in the presence of many witnesses, entrust to faithful men who will be able to teach others also." Find one person to invest in so that the seed that is in you helps someone else grow. Identify someone that you can invest in and let them know that you have been watching them and want to be their mentor in a specific area for a specific timeframe (For example: a year). You will be amazed at the relationships you will build and your gift will open doors for them as well. You will feel pretty good in the process. It feels good to know that your gift is being received, opened, and multiplied.

God's Promise when you use your Gift: Proverbs 18:16 (New American): "A man's gift makes room for him and brings him before great men."

Keep a Victory diary for all the Victories that the Lord gives you. I have kept one since 2003. When you have completed 1 – 3, God has a promise for you; it is our responsibility to live our part and watch God open supernatural doors.

About the Author – Mark Hernandez

Be prepared to be Informed, Challenged, and Inspired to go to a new level of excellence and tap into your inner greatness.

Passion: Mark A. Hernandez lives to equip and empower individuals and organizations in order to Multiply their Purpose and performance.

Multiplication Creed: *Lead Yourself & Multiply Others.*

Chapter 3 – The Gift in You

Inspirational Background:
- Proudly served four years in the US Navy during Desert Storm & Desert Shield,
- Started out as construction scaffold builder,
- First in the Hernandez family to:
  - go to attend college
  - serve as a civil servant 12 years for OSHA,
  - start a business: Multiply Leadership Solutions
  - co-author a book.

Motivational Speaking and Training: Mark harnesses the 20 years of safety experience and the passion to Multiply leaders in order to deliver keynotes and seminars with High Energy, Passion, and Inspiration in order to create a memorable learning experience and a catalyst for change and increase awareness. Mark is a Certified John Maxwell Speaker, Trainer, & Coach.

Key Focus Areas: Motivation, Leadership Development, Transformation, Team effectiveness, Personal & interpersonal effectiveness, Occupational Safety & Health, Bilingual, Seminars & MasterMinds.

Multiplication in Action:
- One keynote, We Is The Key was customized for construction workers and has reached over 6,000 workers,
- 2012 he helped train 10,000 leaders in Guatemala
- 2016 he helped train 15,000 leaders in in Paraguay.

Contact Mark Hernandez:
multiplyleadership@gmail.com
www.johnmaxwellgroup.com/markhernandez

Chapter 3 – The Gift in You

Chapter 4

Move Forward, Pursue Your Dream
By Steve Flores

If I were to ask you if you were living your dream, how would you answer that? If I challenged you and gave you action steps to pursue your dreams, would you embark on that journey?

Many people have life changing dreams, however, very few people pursue their dreams. You can pursue and accomplish your dreams by 'moving forward!' Let those two words become your mantra. This is the driving theme within the mindset of an achiever. I call an achiever one who moves forward in pursuing his/her dreams and is relentless in pursuing that dream to become reality.

One of my favorite quotes growing up as a kid was from Walt Disney, he said: "If you can dream it, you can do it." I hope this chapter not only inspires you but also motivates you to rekindle and fan the flames of your dreams and allow the Holy Spirit to equip, empower & release that dream to become reality in your life. The way I see it, your dream for tomorrow is a gateway to a decision made today! Think about that for a second! I had a dream of being a good husband,

Chapter 4 – Move Forward, Pursue Your Dream

being a loving father, and ensuring that my children are better off than me. That dream was what I was focused on for quite some time. What I failed to discern was that I wasted time dreaming rather than acting upon that dream. I wasted time dreaming instead of praying, seeking mentors, and making bold steps to become a good husband and a present and loving father. I hope you caught the point; a dream is paralyzed without proper action. A dream flourishes like a flower upon the proper watering of action steps. My goal for you, an achiever, is to first re-stimulate, re-energize, and reinforce the God-given dream He has placed upon your heart to fulfill in your life. Secondly, to teach you that your dream is literally a calling of God in your life to help people achieve greater things that in turn will change the world to become a better place. Lastly, I want to warn you that a dream not pursued will erode a sense of purpose and fulfillment in your life.

Unfortunately, we live in a day that embraces dreamers and rarely celebrates achievers. My father had a dream of coming to America to become an American citizen and have his children live in a land of opportunity. My father is a model of an achiever; his actions were louder than his talk. Although many dreamers can inspire many people, they do not always achieve their own dreams. You hear a common language of dreamers that sounds a lot like: "My dream is," "Yeah, one day my dream will come true," "I've had dreams," "If I can accomplish any one dream it would be…" You've heard it, I've heard it, we've all heard it, so now the question at hand is, will you be one of those dreamers that dream or will you be a dreamer that achieves? An achiever

Chapter 4 – Move Forward, Pursue Your Dream

respects the power of a decision that must be made to pursue a dream. I want to be a passionate voice of reassurance for you to pursue your dreams! In this chapter, my prayer for you and my heart's desire is that you have an awakening to a dream that you've put aside or placed on hold. Most who dream are literally paralyzed with fear to move forward with their dreams.

Before I go into depths about this chapter, I will caution you. As you begin your journey to move forward to pursue a dream, you must take into consideration the weight of your decision. If you're ready to make a personal decision to move forward to pursue your dreams, be prepared! Be prepared to face opposition and criticism. You may lose friends and you might feel alone for a season. Rest assured, the new journey paved with grace will forever mark you as a different person. An achiever, and that's what I believe you are right now, is a person desiring to make a difference. Once you've decided to pursue your dreams and you've identified yourself as a successful achiever, then begin in prayer and strategically plan personal quiet times to hear the soft, still voice of the Holy Spirit to guide and empower you. One thing you may have to do is distance yourself from people that are dreamers. Why? Because dreamers will not challenge you to fulfill your dreams. Dreamers will not hold you accountable to pursue your dreams. Dreamers will never encourage you to seek mentors and they will not pray for you. The reality is this – a dreamer has nothing to offer you.

Earlier I shared that we live in a time where we embrace dreamers and we applaud them for their efforts in dreaming,

Chapter 4 – Move Forward, Pursue Your Dream

however we rarely see a celebration of a person achieving a dream. I remember my father sharing with me that when anyone is driven to pursue a dream (in his case, to complete his degree in Psychology), you will be celebrated, you will be honored, and you will be successful in life. My father graduated with honors and was recognized by a local newspaper celebrating with him his great achievement! Now that's an example of an achiever.

As you pursue your dream, you must learn to become painstakingly focused, work hard to eliminate distractions, and be at peace with making sacrifices to witness the fulfillment of your dream to become a reality. Now it's time to dream again and write down your dreams. Know the difference between dreamers and dreaming. Dreamers are people that take no action to see their dream unfold. It's been said that a dream becomes a fairytale when no action steps are pursued. Dreaming is interlaced with praying to seek direction, clarity, and purpose. Again, dreaming is not bad unless you fail to take an action step, which can cause anyone to become a dreamer. Having the knowledge between dreamers and dreaming, it's time to pray to seek and hear God's wonderful grace, wisdom, and instruction. Now it's time to identify distractions. Now it's time to be mentored. Now it's time to embrace accountability. Now it's time to say goodbye to people that do not inspire, motivate, and challenge you in your endeavors. Now is the time to forgive anyone that has hurt you in the past and move forward. Now is the time to focus. Now is the time to end a dead-end relationship that is suffocating your dream. Now is the time to take a leap of faith and witness the grace of God open new

Chapter 4 – Move Forward, Pursue Your Dream

doors of opportunity as He favors you simply because you are His child. Now is the time to believe that your Heavenly Father is a Good God who wants to help you fulfill your dream! Now is the time to take unusual steps of faith and see God take you to soar into effortless success. It is time to end excuses. You see a dream is never a dream until it benefits others first, then in return blesses you!

You may be asking, why is Steve sharing all of these points about accomplishing a dream? Where is he going with this and what is his point? Now the fun begins. Are you ready to pursue your dream? If you find yourself frustrated, stuck, and not going anywhere in life, let's work together to create a plan and become great achievers! But, before you begin your journey to move forward, you must take into consideration the weight of your decision.

In order to move forward to pursue your dream, you will need to make a definitive decision to end certain stalemates. I love to play the great game of chess; it's a game of tactics, strategic thinking, and involves planning ahead to defeat your opponent. Your current choices, much like chess, determine your future. If not played right, your opponent can force you into what all chess masters despise, a forfeited game. This is called a stalemate. In reference to pursuing your dreams, your choices in life can play against you to fail to see your dream unfold and become a reality! Could you be in a current stalemate, where it seems that all the striving, the planning, the advice from people, and the frustrations associated with your desire to see your dream come true, feel

Chapter 4 – Move Forward, Pursue Your Dream

like a stalemate? If so, then let me share with you what I just overcame by identifying four potential stalemates.

To shine light on what a stalemate truly is, it's a stronghold of thinking. A stalemate in reference to pursuing your dream is designed to choke and destroy any dream from moving forward to become reality. As Christians, we are aware of strongholds of thinking. The meaning of a stronghold is a lie that the enemy convinces us is true that becomes a strong, dominating, negative thought that can hold a person's dream hostage. The enemy wants nothing more than an achiever held back by his lies. In order to move forward to pursue your God-given dream, you must discern what I call: "The Four Stalemates." *<u>The four stalemates are: attitudes, mindsets, relationships and environments – in that order</u>*. You have to realize that it could be your choices that are hindering you from being an achiever. We live in a society that blames circumstances, people, and situations rather than owning up to decisions that we've made that have led us to where we are now! However, God's grace is more than enough for you; you can literally start all over and begin to pursue your dreams again.

I want to teach you how to identify these four dangerous stalemates. I'm currently writing a book (that will be released soon) that I will expand upon in greater detail about the blinding effects of stalemates and how they eliminate anyone's potential dreams.

Let us begin to tackle stalemates: our first stalemate is attitudes. At one point in time, I was at a crucial point in my

Chapter 4 – Move Forward, Pursue Your Dream

life when I was aware of severe frustration, damaging boredom, and no opportunities to challenge my personal growth or development where I believed God was taking me in life. This is what I call the tipping point. I knew that the ministry calling and gifts God gave me to become a speaker would comprise of me being a motivator, a teacher/mentor, and an administrative and leadership consultant, what I did not know was when and how. What I painfully realized was that the opportunities to flourish in all of my gifts simply did not present themselves at that time. I became aware of frustration, hurt, and confusion. I then quickly discovered that I began to slowly lose my zeal and passion for life. Here is the crucial point I'm praying that the Holy Spirit will reveal in order to minister healing to you. I remember hearing the enemy whisper in my mind wanting me to develop a bad attitude about that current season that I was at in my life in ministry. The good news is you can be aware of the enemy's tactics when he challenges your attitude to turn sour and to undermine development in your life.

You see, I was a pastor at one point overseeing multiple ministries with great influence and respect that was noticed throughout the church. However, what I was silently fighting within my soul was like a resounding bell that I would shout to God in rage and anger, as I would say, "What about the dream, God, that you placed in me?" I would ask in desperation, "What about the promises that people made to me to give me opportunities to practice the gift of public speaking?" I would constantly ask myself what was wrong with me, why am I being overlooked, why are others given more opportunities than me, and the frustrations, sadness,

Chapter 4 – Move Forward, Pursue Your Dream

and hurt became greater and greater. My attitude became worse and finally, the slippery slope of hopelessness began to creep into my life. I felt as if my dream was dying and that my life was truly dying as well. The dream of becoming a speaker, a motivator, a mentor, and a leadership consultant was literally fading like a rose planted in the desert.

Looking back, I was fighting a negative attitude that was contaminated with cynicism. As I began to hear my language and see my life implode due to my terrible attitude, I gave up and turned to what I do best when I hit a brick wall. I turned my eyes to Jesus the restorer to my soul (Psalm 23) and the healer to my heart and the restoration to my dreams. So, instead of drowning in a sea of bad attitude, I began to pray, read the comforting words found in the scriptures, and asked God for clear direction and insight to my circumstance. Eager to do something drastic, I asked God what steps I should take to begin my journey to fulfill my dreams. Surprisingly enough, God said, "Wait, learn and observe." So, I did just that. I waited with much aggravation and pain for the Lord's next action steps. Do you recall the four stalemates I mentioned earlier? Well, one of those stalemates was attitudes. Bad attitudes can develop in your life when you don't discern the right season to pursue your dreams. Timing is everything. There is a reason a baby is born when it is born, and there is a reason why an airplane becomes airborne when it does. My point is, pursuing your dream must be discerned at the right time! Much like a baby is weak when born prematurely and airplanes crash when forced to take off without enough speed, a dream pursued prematurely can have devastating consequences! Are you experiencing a

Chapter 4 – Move Forward, Pursue Your Dream

stalemate currently due to bad attitudes? If so, allow Jesus to heal you of your bad attitude before you pursue your dream. l had developed a bad attitude due to failure in trusting God's proper timing to pursue my dreams.

In order for me to counteract a bad attitude, I had to remind myself that His dream for me will come to fruition in His way. You see, in order to move forward and step into the fulfillment of your dream, give permission to the Holy Spirit to reveal a bad attitude that could be hindering you. Only Jesus can readjust and change an attitude that is focused on self and He can bring back into focus the purpose behind that dream, meaning your dream will bring honor to God while you serve and help others. A bad attitude can cause you not to learn what God is trying to teach you in your current season in life. I wish someone could have told me, "Steve, God is wanting you to wait, learn, and observe the season you are being developed (and enjoy it) before he catapults you to begin thriving in your calling. Steve, he wants you to master the art of patience before he opens doors for you to live out God's divine purpose for you." I had to learn that the hard way. I masked a terrible attitude. Because of my bad attitude, I did not enjoy what I was doing. I was suffering inside for what seemed to be an eternity. At one moment, I had to seek counseling to shine a light on what was really going on within me. I simply allowed the enemy to make me focus on the future where it caused me to miss the exciting present and now.

The enemy can't touch you, but he sure can speed you up to pursue your dream prematurely and to cause you to miss the

Chapter 4 – Move Forward, Pursue Your Dream

beauty of the here and now. He can cause you to speed up to such a degree that you can prematurely step out of a covering designed to equip, develop and empower you to become mature, so you may, at the right time, close a chapter of your life and begin to write a new chapter. I like to say it this way and I used to preach/teach this often to the crowds while never actually practicing what I was teaching. I hope what I'm about to share with you hits you powerfully, yet inundates you with God's peace and grace. Don't be consumed with what you desire to do in the future that you begin to suffer from all of your current responsibilities now.

After several counseling sessions, much time in prayer and allowing Jesus to heal my bad attitude, I awakened to see the dawn of a new day. I began to enjoy ministry and leading people. I then discovered that there is beauty in waiting while I was being developed. I would say to myself "I'm in the middle of God's will." I began to see the power of God's love heal me from my bad attitude and cause my weary and tired eyes to see my brilliant and wonderful future! Jeremiah 29:11 was stoked again within me and I found myself saying aloud I have a bright future and great hope. No one can move forward to pursue a dream if that person has a bad attitude.

Now that we have tackled one of the four stalemates, attitudes, let's talk about our mindset in relation to our dreams. Your mind has the power to sabotage and hold your dream hostage. Nothing is more damaging than a negative mindset when it comes to pursuing your dreams. What you allow in your mind to linger, especially if it's negative, will

Chapter 4 – Move Forward, Pursue Your Dream

ultimately erode the possibility of moving forward with your dream. I like to say it this way: what you focus on within your mind, paints your future. All of this was me. I became ruthlessly negative in my thinking. My mind was polluted to see the worst in a particular season that God designed for me to develop, to be a unique leader, marked with the success of mastering patience.

A negative mindset can and will destroy any hope to take action. Your mindset can blow away that light at the end of the tunnel. I realized at one point in my life that I became toxic in nature due to my negative mindset. I saw opportunities for spiritual development as a waste of time. I cringed at seeing other people given chances rather than me. I would be upset hearing God remind me to master patience. My prayer life became nonexistent and the people that I was called to lead only became a chore for me to simply check off. I want you to avoid what I just described. Embrace this season of life that you are in right now. Yes, it may seem tough. Yes, it may seem unfair and you may feel frustrated. However, the bottom line is this: allow the Holy Spirit to awaken your new mind that you have in Christ. Allow His mind to renew your thoughts, allow God to whisper to your spirit that this season of waiting is for the sole purpose of learning the beautiful art of, are you ready for this, TRUSTING GOD! When you truly trust God to enable you to pursue your dreams and really hold His hand as He guides you in every decision that must be made, any form of negative thinking will be healed! You will not waste your time playing scenarios in your mind wanting to give so-and-so a piece of your mind, rather, you will simply allow God to

Chapter 4 – Move Forward, Pursue Your Dream

awaken within you, the conscience of a positive, optimistic mindset that will catapult you to pursue your dreams. A negative mindset in relation to pursuing your dream is like a boa constrictor suffocating its prey to death. It's a slow and agonizing death. The enemy wants nothing more to steal your joy by killing your dream through a negative mindset. In my life, I've learned that the human soul can hurt in agony two ways: one is through a tragic event and the other is just as serious, a poisonous negative mindset.

I never knew that my negative mindset hurt my wife, my ministry, and my children. It almost took away His divine calling upon my life. Your calling can be taken out not by the enemy, but by you. I love the scripture that powerfully communicates what you should think about often and constantly. May this minister to you right now, Philippians 4:8: "Finally, whatever is true, whatever is honorable, whatever is just, whatever is pure, whatever is lovely, whatever is commendable, if there is any excellence, if there is anything worthy of praise, think about these things." The Apostle Paul is a great example of remaining painstakingly positive in his thinking while in prison. If he did it in Christ, so can you. Don't waste your time thinking negatively, use that time to thank Jesus for the dream that He will accomplish through you. Remember this point: a dream cannot be pursued if one suffers from a negative mindset.

Let's talk about the stalemate of relationships. Positive relationships are a gift from God. A positive relationship is one that adds meaning, value, purpose, and inspires you to become all that you were destined to become. Throughout

Chapter 4 – Move Forward, Pursue Your Dream

scripture, there are several examples of meaningful relationships and how they should look. Look at the story of Aaron & Moses. Their relationship inspired them to strive to do what's right in the sight of God and it caused them to see the goodness of their friendship. In order to pursue your dream, you must choose your friends wisely. (Proverbs 12:26) If I knew then what I know now, I would have avoided or ended relationships that I thought were a part of my life to help me. I discovered through trial and error that the relationships you have could damage any dream from becoming reality. 1 Corinthians 15:33 says that bad company ruins good morals. What I realized quickly in life is that there is a major difference between a friend and an acquaintance. A friend is one that challenges you to pursue your dream and is always there to encourage you to stay the course, pray, seek wise counsel, and study God's word as you pursue your dream. I never knew that the relationships that I thought were good for me were actually damaging me and the dream that God placed within me. When God gives you a dream, the enemy will send people to sabotage that dream.

If you study the meaning of a friend in the scriptures, you will always find a common theme of encouragement, motivation, and accountability. A friend will always follow up with questions to check in with you to see how you are doing and ask what action steps you are taking. A friend will always share with you that they are praying for you. When a relationship begins to steer you away from God, it's time to move forward and say goodbye to that relationship. A relationship must be hinged upon the grace and the love of God in helping and serving others no matter where life takes

Chapter 4 – Move Forward, Pursue Your Dream

you. You must be careful to choose your relationships wisely. Have you studied the word acquaintance? An acquaintance is someone who really does not know you, however, they have strong opinions of what you should do or not do. It's like a perfect stranger that you meet at Starbucks who starts talking to you about finances, then you share your dream about opening a business, then he shoots you down for having that idea and overwhelms you with facts and statistics on how your dream cannot happen. Why bother with people like that? Relationships are so strategic in life that having the wrong ones can cause you to simply walk away from a divine dream God has called you to. Look back at a moment in your life and ask yourself, "What relationships have I moved forward from that have made me a better person?" How about this question, "What relationships am I better off not being involved with?"

Years ago, I began to seek counsel to inquire and take inventory of my friends, only to painfully discover that they were not friends, they were just acquaintances. Instead of what I thought of as friends encouraging me to pursue my dreams, I noticed my relationships at that time simply talked more about negative subject matters. I painfully realized that my relationships were not in my best interest; it seemed clearer to me that they cared more about their world and never once inquired how I was doing nor asked me where God was taking me. Please take this point to heart: you must take into consideration your relationships. Healthy relationships talk about life, how to overcome the challenges associated with life, point you to Jesus, partner with you in your success, pray for and with you, and lastly, they hold you

Chapter 4 – Move Forward, Pursue Your Dream

accountable to pursue your dreams. The litmus test of genuine relationships is that of accountability as you pursue your dreams. Today I still enjoy meaningful relationships that hold me accountable to pursue my dreams. I have had to move forward from damaging relationships to embrace Christ-centered friendships. The enemy cannot stand a person that has a dream given to them by God. Could it be that you're being blindsided and hindered from pursuing your dreams by certain relationships? Only you know that. I believe right now that the Holy Spirit is revealing who or whom you should move forward with and begin to see the light of what a Christ-centered relationship should be. It's time to move forward to pursue your dream! Remember this point: your dream can be hindered or taken out by having the wrong relationships in your life!

Are you excited about the journey you have read in this chapter and do you feel you're making progress? Do you sense the Holy Spirit empower you to move forward with the dream he has placed within you? I pray you do!

Now, it's time to tackle the final stalemate: the stalemate of environments. A fertilized egg, before it miraculously becomes a baby for delivery, must be developed in an environment within the mother's womb for growth, incubation, and health before that baby enters the world. An environment is your direct circle of influence. Basically, it's people who you allow to speak into your life. You are an achiever; you are designed by God to succeed. You will accomplish your dream and you must realize and ask God if

Chapter 4 – Move Forward, Pursue Your Dream

your environment is suffocating your dream from becoming reality.

It has been said that it takes a village to raise a child, and the same can be said about an achiever. One must be around achievers in order to succeed! An achiever should make a high priority to surround themselves with winners! Your direct circle of influence (your environment) should be a genuine model of success. They should speak the truths of God's promises over you. They should be the ones that usher you into a season of development, trust, and accountability. The environment that you surround yourself with should constantly be a resounding source of wisdom, optimism, positivity, prayer, encouragement, and correction, all while interlaced with the truths of God's grace found in His word. Your environment should be a safe place of vulnerability where you can share personal struggles and receive correction and guidance without feeling guilty, shameful, or condemned. It should be a place of constant encouragement paralleled with correction.

When an environment is without correction, it becomes a place of rebellion. When you become focused to pursue your dream, it will be marked with learning new things, being challenged, and accepting accountability. These things will be embraced and taught as a point to succeed. An environment without the points I mentioned above is not a healthy environment for personal development. A dream will never become reality without a healthy environment of development. In your environment, are you being challenged to seek God for direction? Are you pointed to the unending

Chapter 4 – Move Forward, Pursue Your Dream

resources that you have in Christ? Are you being taught about the grace of God? The wrong environment can destroy a dream.

To this day, I still lean on some incredible men and women of God that I've known for more than a decade. They always point me to Jesus, God's promises found in His word, and the beauty of praying and enjoying the effortless unforced rhythms of God's timing! The wrong environment will point you to self, doing things your own way rather than enjoying the process of developing before God elevates you to pursue your dreams. Timing is everything. The wrong environment can kill God's dream for you. You must be aware of your environment. Do you feel refreshed, challenged, or motivated after you've spent time in your environment? If not, it's time to move forward from that environment and allow God to bring the right environment to you as you experience His grace empowering you. I'll give you an example of a powerful environment. Study the environment of the Apostle Peter. The foundation of his legacy was in his environment that challenged him and motivated him as he flourished as a leader because that environment embraced accountability. Peter was in a circle of influence with Jesus and the men that Christ would choose to bring change that the world needed. He was a part of the twelve disciples and became a pioneer of Christianity that Jesus would describe as "the rock from which I will build my church." The right environment will flourish you, equip you, empower you, and release you to walk forth in your dream. Remember this point: the wrong environment (circle of influence) can destroy your God-given dream.

Chapter 4 – Move Forward, Pursue Your Dream

Are you ready to move forward? Are you ready to make some changes in your life? Are you aware of what the Holy Spirit is revealing to you? Do you believe that you are an achiever? Believe you are!

My prayer for you is that Jesus would shine light upon the four stalemates that you may be going through. I want to leave you with some simple action steps to get you on the proper path to execute, to move forward, and to pursue your dream. Remember, a genuine, God-given dream will always bless other people first, then bless you in return as the people you've impacted make this world a better place. As we close this chapter, I ask you to open your mind, heart, and soul to Jesus for direction, healing, and purpose.

Questions to consider. Take the time to really ask yourself the tough questions. Take time alone with God in a quiet place and ask the Holy Spirit to help you answer these questions truthfully. If you desire to make this world a better place and really desire God to fill your life with purpose and excitement, then take your time with the following questions and write them down on a sheet of paper or in your journal. I did and my life has never been the same.

Is my attitude good or bad?
Do I have a negative mindset?
Are certain relationships harmful to me?
Do I need to change my environment?

Now that you have asked yourself some tough questions, it is time to develop an action plan. Some say that a dream

Chapter 4 – Move Forward, Pursue Your Dream

without a plan of action is a waste of time. A dream is marked with a plan of action in order to succeed. Before moving towards a plan of action, ask God to bring the right people and environment into your life that can partner with you to succeed. As you write your plan on paper, expect Jesus to bring the right people to develop, mentor, and hold you accountable to your action plan. Lastly, be open-minded with what God reveals to you as you begin to move into your action plan. Don't be surprised if God asks you to do things in an unusual way! God works wonders in our lives that seem unusual to some.

Action Steps:
How can I change my attitude?

How can I change my mindset?
What are the relationships that I must move forward from?
What environments do I need to change?

Feel free to contact me for personal mentorship, guidance, or to develop action plans to move forward to pursue your dream.

I'll leave you with this: an idea becomes a passion, that passion gives birth to a dream, your dream unlocks purpose, and your purpose awakens your calling!

Move forward and pursue your dream!

Chapter 4 – Move Forward, Pursue Your Dream

About the Author – Steve Flores

Steve Flores can empower organizations and individuals to achieve long lasting and productive goals. He is a dynamic and passionate communicator who helps guide and teach organizations to meet the challenges of staying ahead while being relevant. His teaching abilities range from leadership development to administrative skills. His unique method of connecting with people individually or in a teaching environment has led him to be known as a "people's person."

Steve's current career as an Administrative Specialist at State Farm corporate has led him to receive numerous team recognitions regarding his efficient and effective work ethic. Recently at State Farm he has been recognized for his gift to bring people together in a team environment and he has won an award for exceptional customer service.

Steve also serves as a pastor at Calvary Church. During his 10-year tenure of full time ministry at Calvary he has built a large hospitality ministry of volunteers while overseeing a leadership development program that has graduated over 300 alumni. Steve is known for mentoring people that desire to be leaders in ministry or in the corporate setting.

Chapter 4 – Move Forward, Pursue Your Dream

He thrives in teaching the art of equipping people or organizations to set and execute goals, eliminate high turnover, manage time effectively, re-strategize to re-build leadership in the home, church or corporate environment. Under the mentorship of Steve Flores, individuals or organizations can achieve great results that are consistent. Steve models what he teaches.

Contact information:
Instagram: @steveflores10
Twitter: @steveAflores
Linked-In: Steve Flores
email: stevef@calvarychurch.cc

Chapter 4 – Move Forward, Pursue Your Dream

Chapter 5

A Life Well Lived
By Mark Turner

I had known about him since I was a kid, but my real interactions started taking place at the age of 17 when I began dating his oldest daughter.

To most in the community, he held the reputation of a great businessman and a great community leader. His involvement in being elected to various leadership positions on boards coupled with his dedication to a perfect attendance record with the Rotary Club kept him in the public eye. While building a wonderful business and raising a family, he was endowed with the heart of a servant.

My journey with him would bless me in numerous ways and in fashions that continue to show up even today. Just when I think the lessons are over, something happens and a new revelation occurs. We each have impactful people we encounter on our journeys and I want to share this man with you and provide you some of his insights that, if you choose to follow them, will enhance your life.

Chapter 5 – A Life Well Lived

Glynn Ellis became my father in-law on July 26, 1980. I realize as I write this that quite a few people have struggles with in-laws after they marry. My life and my experience was not that way. I am grateful that Glynn became another father to me. What an awesome privilege I had to be his son in-law. He never let the words 'in-law' get in-between our relationship and he treated me like a son.

His life started in rural East Texas in the town of Edgewood. He and his two brothers grew up in a time where there was no money and lived in a house that, at one point, had dirt floors. He grew into a fine young man and joined the Marines at an early age.

Following his time in the Marines, Glynn returned home and married his lifelong love, June (whom we all call Momma June) and made their home in Wills Point, Texas. He found his career start in the shoe business by being a traveling shoe salesman. Sensing a market void in the small communities nearby, he opened Fairway Shoe Store in Wills Point, Texas. Fairway Shoes would become the largest family owned and operated shoe store in the South.

Glynn had a business mind for opportunity and together with his cousin Norman and some close friends, they started a bank that eventually grew to three branches. He purchased real estate in the residential and commercial markets. Most would say that Glynn had the 'Midas Touch.'

Glynn was a giant of a man in stature and personality and to a young man in 1980 he seemed larger than life.

Chapter 5 – A Life Well Lived

Glynn was a true servant in every form of the word. He served God, he served the church, he served his family, he served his community, and he served the needy.

Through his heart for the Lord, Glynn devoted time to ensuring that things in the community of Wills Point were taken care of. His leadership abilities were clear and as such, people naturally migrated toward him when it came to hurdles that needed to be surmounted. While his eyes were on the lookout for ways to help, his heart directed his actions.

Philippians 2:3-4 states, "Let nothing be done through selfish ambition or conceit, but in lowliness of mind let each esteem others better than himself. Let each of you look out not only for his own interests, but also for the interests of others." (NKJV)

Glynn looked out for the interest of others and placed others first, not only in word but also in deed.

One thing everybody knew shortly after meeting Glynn was that he was so proud to have served his country and was especially proud to be a Marine. In fact, he planned many years in advance to be buried in his Marine uniform.

Article VI. of the United States Marine Corp Code of Conduct states, "I will never forget that I am an American, fighting for freedom, responsible for my actions, and dedicated to the principles which made my country free. I will trust in my God and in the United States of America."

Chapter 5 – A Life Well Lived

These principles were part of the foundation of Glynn's character. And rest assured, his trust was in God.

The story is told that while serving as a Marine in Korea in the Inchon Valley on Thanksgiving one year, Glynn decided that the standard rations would not suffice for a proper dinner. He decided to sneak into the buffer zone and shoot some pheasant. Having grown up hunting and fishing in East Texas, Glynn was quite familiar with the process and decided he could use this experience to supply a great meal for his buddies in camp.

He took a rifle and started his trek into the no man's land. As he snuck out and got further and further from camp, he didn't realize that he became a target to the North Koreans. As he hunted his prey, the enemy marked him as their prey. The North Koreans began firing shells from a cannon to his location. The first explosion scared the wits out of him. You can rest assured that he never ran as fast in a zigzag pattern in his entire life as he did that day.

His heart of wanting to serve his friends and comrades almost cost him his very life that day.

Perhaps the biggest impact he had on me and countless others was his walking example of a Christian life. His love of people led him to help many individuals and families over several decades. His love of the church led him to become an Elder. His love of the Word led him to invite every person he met to attend church with him.

Chapter 5 – A Life Well Lived

I had a gentleman tell me of the time he was young and his family was impoverished and his mother couldn't afford shoes for the children or herself. He said Glynn would show up at their house with boxes of shoes for him, his siblings, and his mother. Glynn would fit each of them right there at home as if they were going to the store. He said that never once did Glynn ever mention it, and to my knowledge, this was the first time it was ever told. Glynn had a way of doing exactly what the Bible said in Matthew 6:3-4, "But when you do a charitable deed, do not let your left hand know what your right hand is doing, that your charitable deed may be in secret; and your Father who sees in secret will Himself reward you openly." I would find this same type of scenario repeated to me by others. Glynn's heart of a servant was done in secret.

Rather than simply hand out money, Glynn would find work for people in need. He would often have folks working for him on his farm or in one of his warehouses. He believed that someone would be better benefitted from working and it would build them up. He also took every opportunity to invite them to church. Most who worked for Glynn at some point also occupied a pew with him during worship.

Glynn would let people live in a cabin he built if they needed a place to stay. He let one young man live for almost two years in a travel trailer right beside his house as he got back on his feet.

His heart was centered around Matthew 25:31-35, "When the Son of Man comes in His glory, all the holy angels with Him, then He will sit on the throne of His glory. All the nations will be gathered before Him, and He will separate them one from another, as a shepherd divides his sheep from the goats. And He will set the sheep on His right hand, but the goats on the left. Then the King will say to those on His right hand, 'Come, you blessed of My Father, inherit the kingdom prepared for you from the foundation of the world: for I was hungry and you gave Me food; I was thirsty and you gave Me drink; I was a stranger and you took Me in; I was naked and you clothed Me; I was sick and you visited Me; I was in prison and you came to Me.'"

Glynn saw the hungry and fed them, saw the thirsty and gave them drink. This Scripture represented his life. His heart was always on the lookout for someone to serve.

My wife, Cathy, was visiting with an elderly woman one day and somewhere in their discussion the woman asked Cathy if she liked her TV. Cathy told her she did and the woman said, "Your daddy gave that to me." Another example of giving and serving without anyone knowing. Only the Lord knows how many of these examples exist.

I found a small calendar book with many blank pages that Glynn carried in his pocket wherever he went. This small book was a constant companion and a place for him to write short notes on his thoughts. The most prominent thing in the book was the dog-eared pages where there were two scriptures he had written down:

Matthew 28:18-20 states, "And Jesus came and spoke to them, saying, 'All authority has been given to Me in heaven and on earth. Go therefore and make disciples of all the

Chapter 5 – A Life Well Lived

nations, baptizing them in the name of the Father and of the Son and of the Holy Spirit, teaching them to observe all things that I have commanded you; and lo, I am with you always, even to the end of the age.'" (NKJV)

Mark 12:29-31 says, "Jesus answered him, 'The first of all the commandments is: Hear, O Israel, the Lord our God, the Lord is one. And you shall love the Lord your God with all your heart, with all your soul, with all your mind, and with all your strength. This is the first commandment. And the second, like it, is this: 'You shall love your neighbor as yourself. There is no other commandment greater than these.'" (NKJV)

I believe it was a constant reminder, every time he opened that small book, what his true mission on earth was about.

Glynn's heart of service was always apparent in his devotion to Momma June and his kids.

He understood and lived the scripture in Ephesians 5:25-33 which says, "Husbands, love your wives, just as Christ also loved the church and gave Himself for her, that He might sanctify and cleanse her with the washing of water by the word, that He might present her to Himself a glorious church, not having spot or wrinkle or any such thing, but that she should be holy and without blemish. So husbands ought to love their own wives as their own bodies; he who loves his wife loves himself. For no one ever hated his own flesh, but nourishes and cherishes it, just as the Lord does the church. For we are members of His body, of His flesh and of His bones. 'For this reason a man shall leave his father and mother and be joined to his wife, and the two shall become one flesh.' This is a great mystery, but I speak concerning Christ and the church. Nevertheless let each of you in particular so love his own wife as himself, and let the wife see that she respects her husband."

Glynn served his family daily and set an example for his children and the extended family like me.

Outside of his business dealings and leadership positions in the community, one of the things I remember about Glynn is his blue eyes. As you sat and talked with him, you could see the emotions of the conversation in his eyes. When you were discussing scripture, he would take on an intense, focused look as he listened intently while his brain whizzed away. Telling childhood stories, his eyes would light up and dance about, which only served to make the stories that much better. When he would greet his children, family, or anyone else for that matter, his eyes sparkled and you felt important. When his grown children would sit in his lap, his eyes showed a depth of love and thanksgiving only a dad can truly understand. It is said that the eyes are a gateway to the soul. Glynn's eyes revealed a soul that was rooted in love.

In 2011, Glynn was diagnosed with Alzheimer's disease. It came as a blow to him and the family, but also provided the explanation for everyone why things with him had changed over the last year.

At first, there were very small signs. In hindsight, it was evident what was occurring, but at that moment the puzzle pieces were not put together. Forgetting names is something

Chapter 5 – A Life Well Lived

we all do, so we don't notice it right away. When we don't get enough sleep or have too many plates spinning in our lives, we forget things and don't place much emphasis on it, which is why it took some time for the pieces of the puzzle to fit. Glynn would have some difficulty coming up with the right word at times. Again, not something that is noticed in the moment. He would ask the same question that you answered yesterday and would not remember that he had already asked you. He also developed issues with money handling – something he had always been very good at.

As the Alzheimer's progressed, his personality changed slightly for a period as his frustration increased. How difficult it must be to know that you don't know. It was at this stage that Glynn's trust in people increased while his discernment decreased. He constantly had people wanting to borrow money accompanied with the promise of payback only to be pinched by these unscrupulous individuals. His heart of serving was still at work when the disease was dimming his view.

Time was something he could control and it exhibited itself in routine. His days as a Marine set within him the importance of time and punctuality. Time became a last frontier of control for Glynn. When the clock hit 8:30p.m. on the nose, it was time for bed every night, regardless of what was going on. But with the disease, sleep patterns changed. Eating patterns changed. This roller coaster of a disease was slowly ebbing away the Glynn that I knew.

In the final stages, Glynn required around-the-clock care and assistance with his daily personal life. He had lost awareness

Chapter 5 – A Life Well Lived

of recent experiences and referred to everyone as "my friend" since he could not recall their names. The change within his mind had not affected his body until this point and I witnessed a weakness slowly overtake him. That strong Marine was weakening before my eyes and it was heartbreaking to watch.

There are many stories of people becoming combative during this process and to be honest, it was something that I had feared. How would we help someone as big in stature as Glynn if he became aggressive? While my mind thought of this often, I fully forgot about the heart of the man. Glynn's life had been spent in service and that heart belonged to God. That heart would drive him and triumph over any direction Alzheimer's had planned.

Over the next three years, those active eyes began to lose some of their light as Alzheimer's took over. Looking at his eyes, you would see that something inside of him knew that he should know you, but he couldn't quite figure out why he didn't. However, the heart behind the eyes remained true. While Glynn could not remember his children's names, that Momma June was his wife, what day it was, or what time meant, he was still able to show how the Word is engraved on someone's heart. The heart behind those eyes still shone brightly.

Whenever someone would assist him in getting out of a chair he always replied, "Thank you." Whenever someone would hug him or give him a kiss on the cheek, he always replied, "I love you." "Thank you" and "I love you." I will never understand how the mind works under these conditions, but

Chapter 5 – A Life Well Lived

it is clear how the heart works. Glynn called everything a "unit" because he couldn't think of the words but these two phrases remained with him regardless of what Alzheimer's threw at him.

The seeds of the Word were planted firmly in Glynn's heart. The heart behind the eyes was steeped in gratitude and love.

I don't know why Alzheimer's exists. I don't fully understand God's plan for it. I do know that I acquired so much from the experience and blessing of being Glynn's son in-law. I believe that every relative and friend associated with his family were blessed with his life. I reflect often on the gains in life I have been fortunate enough to acquire through his example.

I gained a new appreciation for what other people experience. It helped to place me in a mindset of taking me out of the picture and putting others first. Mark 9:35 says, "And He sat down, called the twelve, and said to them, 'If anyone desires to be first, he shall be last of all and servant of all.'" Glynn lived a life where others came first. His heart drove his eyes to remain on the lookout for someone to serve. I look forward with anticipation as I know more stories about the lives he had touched that are yet to be told. Our prayer each day should be that God provides us with the opportunity to serve.

I gained a renewed respect for the aged among us. The day-to-day struggles of aging were witnessed on the front line by the entire family. I personally witnessed how the obstacles were faced with a lot of patience on the part of family and

Chapter 5 – A Life Well Lived

caretakers and grace on behalf of Glynn. I saw where the dedication of how loving children rose to the greatest heights. My heart and my understanding was changed. We see elderly people or people with health difficulties daily and it is too easy to dismiss the struggle they are facing. Watching this family and the host of caretakers pour their lives into Glynn truly humbled me.

I gained a thankfulness that I was able to know and love a great man. A man who remained great in my eyes while in the depths of Alzheimer's. It has given me an insight into this disease and an understanding when I encounter people today that may be experiencing the same thing. My approach today is so different from where I was and I am better for it. Love is the driving force that creates the patience, the empathy, the action, the compassion, the kindness, and the sensitivity that is required during circumstances such as these.

I gained a thankfulness for the lessons of life he taught me over the years. Lessons I still utilize in business today. Lessons like the time a man came in the shoe store and brought a pair of boots back to exchange for a new pair. Glynn gave him his money and told him to never come back to his store again. I questioned him on the harshness of this exchange and he told me, "Son, that man has brought three pair of boots back after wearing each for one month and got a new pair each time. Let me tell you, there are some people in this world whose business you can't afford." I have used that one lesson in many leadership and business seminars.

Chapter 5 – A Life Well Lived

I gained the importance of providing an example to your children. Glynn's total devotion to God and the church and the priority he placed there was a guiding path for me. The kids tell stories of them traveling on vacation. The family pulled a travel trailer and regardless of where they were at the moment, Glynn would pull over on Sunday and they would have church on the side of the road. He loved the church and absolutely believed that we need to be together on Sunday to encourage each other in God's Word.

I gained the understanding that a tenacious drive can be coupled with a loving heart to ensure the best outcome in any situation. Glynn could be bull-headed and when his eyes were set on a prize, he would pursue it with great intensity. However, he always kept the individual in mind. He would never intentionally hurt anyone and if he thought someone would be enticed to stumble in their walk with God, he would rather not have the business deal.

Lastly, I gained the understanding that priorities matter. Glynn's priorities were God, family, and friends, in that exact order. We live in a society today where we are bombarded daily with the exact opposite of this. Glynn didn't let anything get in his way of his relationship with God. God was always first. When he could not remember what day it was, he would ask the question on a daily basis, "How many days until we go to church?" That question became, "How long until I get to go out there where those people are?" When Cathy and I got to pick him up on Sunday mornings, he would be ready hours before we got there. God was first.

Chapter 5 – A Life Well Lived

Acts 13:36-37 says, "For David, after he had served his own generation by the will of God, fell asleep, was buried with his fathers, and saw corruption, but He whom God raised up saw no corruption."

On March 30, 2015, Glynn Ellis fell asleep and went home to be with the Lord. It is my prayer that his example be found in every one of us. May each of us have our eyes on the constant lookout for opportunities to serve and may our hearts be grounded in the Word.

About the Author – Mark Turner

Mark Turner is a lifelong resident of Wills Point, Texas. He has been married to Cathy for over 36 years and they have two wonderful children, Grant and Katie.

Mark has spent his entire career in the communication's sector in technical and leadership positions. He has lived abroad and traveled extensively during his career.

Chapter 5 – A Life Well Lived

Most recently, Mark was the President and Chief Operating Officer of Value-Added Communications (VAC). VAC was sold to its largest competitor several years ago and Mark continued as a consultant for a three-year period until deciding to become a full-time speaker and trainer. Mark is the founder of a motivational, business-building and personal improvement company named N2Success.

Mark has taught Bible Class for over 30 years and preaches many times a year at his home church. He is a Ziglar Certified Speaker and Trainer and a Certified Human Behavior Consultant with Personality Insights Institute. Inspiring leadership and propelling relationships to greatness are passionate areas Mark covers in his keynote addresses and training. Mark loves to provide training using the D.I.S.C. Model of Human Behavior. He says, "Where else can people have so much fun, learn so much insight into themselves and improve every relationship they have all in one session?"

Mark can be reached at mark@n2success.com.

Chapter 5 – A Life Well Lived

Chapter 6

Are You Fully Equipped?
By Mike Rodriguez

Most people don't think about the beginning of their life this way, but on the day that you were born, it was just you and God. Yes, your mother was there as a vessel to give birth and a doctor was there as a resource, but it was only you and God when the journey of your life started. God gave you everything you need to succeed in this world. I'll prove it as you walk through this with me:
What clothing were you born wearing? None.
What material possessions did you have when you were born? None.

In fact, when you were born, you didn't have anything except God. It was only you and Him and what He equipped you with for your life. He provided you with eyes to see, ears to hear and a nose and lungs to breathe. You probably have two arms, two hands and ten fingers to grasp, two legs to walk and two feet to stand. God gave you a mouth to talk and eat, a digestive system, a reproductive system, an immune system, a heart to keep you alive and even complex brain tissue for you to think, feel and be. He gave you all of your personal resources, for His purposes for YOUR life.

Know that God doesn't make mistakes.
God gave you everything you need to succeed in this world. If you don't or didn't have any of the mentioned body parts, then that is a part of His purpose for your life as well. You were born prepared for His plans for your life. It is a truth that most of us never really think about because we tend to mess things up. We do this by adding negative things that He never gave us or even intended for us to have. We add these things, then we falsely define them as a part of who we are.

We are born perfect in God's eyes, fully prepared to succeed, but along the way, we lose sight of whose we are and what we're capable of achieving through and with Him. Life happens to us and we start engaging in bad or unhealthy things. We might begin to abuse alcohol or drugs. We might start getting angry, depressed, or create unhealthy addictions, thoughts or actions. Sometimes we completely redefine who we think we are, due to the confusion and deception in this world. However, God's message is very clear: You have *A Bigger Purpose* and He has already equipped you for that purpose. You just need to own it and accept who He created you to be.

When you were born, do you remember that tag made of flesh attached to your side? You know, the one that said, "addict," "depressed," "anger issues," "fearful," "worried," "confused" or something else that was negative?

Chapter 6 – Are You Fully Equipped?

No, you say? You don't remember having that or even being born with an extra flesh tag with a negative description of yourself? Of course not, because it wasn't there.

The reason it wasn't there, is because God never put it there! This is the part where you might say, but Mike, I do have a defining negative characteristic and it is a part of me, but I've always been that way! This is where I tell you that you are wrong. God never gave you any negative defining characteristics. That was all your doing.

Living in a world dominated by sin, causes us to sin. Sometimes, we can sin so much and for so long that we can get confused and accept the sin as our own identity. We can confuse what we DO, as who we are. I challenge you to accept and believe that the things you DO, really aren't who you are. I'm not talking about shirking responsibility for your actions, I am talking about separating what God made you to be, versus what you have added to your life through what you DO. If you are doing things you shouldn't be doing, stop doing them! Once you stop doing those things, you will remove from your life what you brought in or introduced. God never intended those things to be there in the first place.

Sometimes, we do negative and sinful things for so long that we can cover ourselves in those things, hiding who we truly are. When diamonds are mined from the earth, the seekers can be deceived as they sort through thick chunks of carbon. However, if they can keep their eyes on the prize, not on the nasty carbon, the seekers can and usually will find the brilliant gems inside, covered by the years of darkness. It can be difficult to sort through thick layers of dark decay. It requires great work to remove the layers of carbon to reveal the brilliance of the beautiful diamond inside.

Our lives with Christ are similar to mining diamonds.
God has given us His brilliant, shining light to be found inside. The challenge is that some of us have hidden the brilliant light within, by covering ourselves with layers of dark carbon, represented by years of sinful nature, negative actions, and habits. Some of us have been sinning for so long that we have falsely accepted the layers of carbon as a part of who we are. When we do this, we allow the layers of darkness to prevent God's brilliant light within us from shining to the rest of the world.

The great news is that although you may not feel like you can remove the years of negativity or darkness that you may be trapped in, God loves you and He can! He makes all things new! He can help you remove the years of negative and sinful things that have been hiding His light inside of you!

Yes, you and God started your life journey and it will be just you and God who will end your life journey together, if you know Him. Will you be prepared to give an account of what you did according to His plans for your life?

You can be prepared right now.
Here is how:

Chapter 6 – Are You Fully Equipped?

The Bible says that the only way to know God is through Jesus. In fact, Jesus said, "I am the way, the truth, and the life. No one can come to the Father except through me." John 14: 6.

This means that by asking Jesus into your life, you can know God. In your own words, pray and repent of your sins and confess that you believe Jesus died for your sins on the cross. Acknowledge Jesus Christ as your Lord and Savior and ask Him into your heart.

If you said this prayer on your own free will right now, then congratulations, you have been saved and you are fully equipped! Praise God.
However, you need to continue to do your part and live your life in a way that honors God.

Now go forth and make your life exceptional!

- Mike Rodriguez

MikeRodriguezInternational.com

Chapter 6 – Are You Fully Equipped?

Chapter 6 – Are You Fully Equipped?

A Bigger Purpose – Stories That Inspire

EPILOGUE

Throughout my life, I have always felt a bigger and better purpose for my life, but I have not always been in pursuit of it, mostly because I have been my own biggest obstacle. I was often distracted by my current comfort zones through my current routines. They kept me from stepping into my full potential and kept me as a prisoner to mediocrity. I knew that I wanted to pursue my "bigger purpose," I just wasn't focused enough to see it or empowered enough to take action.

After years of very strong feelings that God had something better for me, I only took action to start changing my life, when I chose to have faith and act on God's plan for me. I knew this was the only way to make bigger things happen.

Through His grace, I am a new man. I understand my purpose and I am full of life. I can see Him clearly, and I am stronger than ever.

With regard to success, I have always felt that my purpose was to help others through the gift of speaking. I have always dreamed of becoming a motivational/inspirational speaker, but for the largest part of my life, I only considered this a dream.
Who was I to be a speaker?
What credentials or gifts did I have?
These were negative thoughts that I burdened myself with.

So, who am I?
I am a son of our King.
I know Him and He knows me.

Today, all because of Him, and through my obedience to decide, take action and have faith, I am living my life's dream. I am pursuing my life's goal, and most importantly, my life's purpose to help others build their lives all for the glory of God.

Believe in God and His plan for your life. Have faith and take action. You too can realize your bigger purpose as the son or daughter of the same King!

Now Go Forth and Make YOUR Life Exceptional!

- **Mike Rodriguez**

A Bigger Purpose – Stories That Inspire

A Bigger Purpose – Stories That Inspire

About Mike Rodriguez

Mike Rodriguez is CEO of Mike Rodriguez International, LLC, a professional speaking, training and global ministry organization. Besides being a Best-Selling author, he is an international motivator and a leadership and sales expert. Mike and his wife Bonnie also own a publishing company and they still manage to spend quality time with their five daughters, all while Mike is studying for his master's degree at Dallas Theological Seminary (as of 2017). Mike is a former showcase speaker with the original Zig Ziglar Corporation and was selected as their key speaker for the 2015 Ziglar U.S. Tour.

Mike delivers performance-based seminars and trainings and has authored several books which have been promoted by Barnes & Noble. He has been featured on CBS, U.S. News & World Report, Success Magazine and he has lectured at Baylor University, UNT and K-State Research. His clients include names like Hilton, McDonald's Corporation and the Federal Government. As a people expert, Mike has trained thousands around the world.

Everyone faces challenges; Mike believes that through faith and action, you can overcome the challenges in your life to attain your goals and become who God has called you to be.

Mike has been happily married since 1991 to Bonnie, the love of his life and together they have five beautiful daughters. He believes if you have the right attitude and the right faith, you can have the right kind of success, regardless of the type of industry that you are in.

A Bigger Purpose – Stories That Inspire

A Bigger Purpose – Stories That Inspire

As a world-renowned speaker,
Mike has experience working with people
from all walks of life.

You can schedule Mike Rodriguez
to speak, inspire or train at your next event.
Go to:
www.MikeRodriguezInternational.com

Other books available by Mike Rodriguez:

Finding Your WHY

8 Keys to Exceptional Selling

Break Your Routines to Fix Your Life

Lion Leadership

Think BIG Motivational Quotes

The Power of Breaking Routines
(Audio Course from Nightingale Conant)

Walking with Faith

A Bigger Purpose – Stories That Inspire

A Bigger Purpose – Stories That Inspire

A Bigger Purpose – Stories That Inspire

A Bigger Purpose – Stories That Inspire

Disclaimer & Copyright Information

Some of the events, locales, and conversations have been recreated from memories. In order to maintain their anonymity, in some instances, the names of individuals and places have been changed. As such, some identifying characteristics and details may have changed.

Although the authors and publishers have made every effort to ensure that the information in this book was correct at press time, the authors and publishers do not assume and hereby disclaim any liability to any party for any loss, damage, or disruption caused by errors or omissions, whether such errors or omissions result from negligence, accident, or any other cause. Each author is responsible for the content of each story.

All quotes, unless otherwise noted,
are attributed to the respective Authors or to the Holy Bible.

Cover illustration, book design and production
Copyright © 2017 by Tribute Publishing LLC
www.TributePublishing.com

"Go Forth and Make Your Life Exceptional" ™
is a copyrighted trademark of the Author, Mike Rodriguez.

Scripture references are copyrighted by www.BibleGateway.com
which is operated by the Zondervan Corporation, L.L.C

A Bigger Purpose – Stories That Inspire

*"I can do ALL THINGS through Christ
who strengthens me."
Philippians 4:13*

NOTES

NOTES

NOTES

www.ingramcontent.com/pod-product-compliance
Lightning Source LLC
Chambersburg PA
CBHW021130300426
44113CB00006B/362